(´)   The primary accent mark is used after the syllable requiring the heaviest stress.

(ʹ)   The secondary accent mark is used after a syllable requiring a lighter stress than the primary accent mark but more stress than a syllable with no accent mark.

(ˉ)   The macron is used to mark long vowels. Long vowels are pronounced at face value a e i o or u as in fāke, ēve, īce, nō, use.

(˘)   The breve is used to mark short vowels. Short vowels are pronounced as follows:

> ă măp
> ĕ mĕt
> ĭ ĭt
> ŏ hŏt
> ŭ ŭp
>
> For simplication the short vowels will not show the breve in this book.

(ˆ)   The circumflex has three uses:

> 1. Over the o(ô) it indicates the sound of o in ôr, ôrder and côrn.
> 2. Over the u(û) it indicates the sound of u in tûrn and hûrt.
> 3. Over the a(â) it indicates the sound of a in âir and bâre.

(··)   The dieresis is placed over the vowel a (ä) to give it a broad sound as in fäther and bärb.

(o͞o)  The double o with the wide macron is pronounced as in fo͞ol and bo͞oze.

(o͝o)  The double o with the wide breve is pronounced as in bo͝ok and to͝ok.

# Big Words for Big Shooters

# Big Words

## FOR

# Big Shooters

### JOHN E. ROSE, JR.

NEW YORK  EVEREST HOUSE  PUBLISHERS

Library of Congress in Publication Data

Rose, John E., Jr.
  Big words for big shooters.

  1. Vocabulary.   I. Title
PE1449.R675              428.1              82-1555
ISBN 0-89696-151-6                          AACR2

*to Mom and Dad*

Special thanks to Louise Sanderson
of Oakland University, Marquita Andinion
of Oakland schools, and Carolyn Kazen for editorial
and advisory assistance.

# INTRODUCTION

Why are you interested in vocabulary expansion? There are, obviously, many good reasons, and one of the following is undoubtedly yours:

1. You may be tired of facing a daily barrage of mysterious words, the meaning of which you are completely ignorant. If these are important descriptive words, you will have a poor understanding of the context in which they appear. Thus, better comprehension is your primary motivation for vocabulary improvement.

2. You may want to enhance your communication skills. It is true that the more words you have in your memory warehouse, the less pausing and groping you'll go through to find that *perfect* word, the one that fits smoothly and meaningfully. In addition, the more command and control you have of words, the more you will be respected and appreciated as a conversationalist, speaker, and writer. Realizing that communication skills are valuable and important as both a business and a social asset, you naturally want to place heavy emphasis upon their cultivation and growth.

3. You may want a larger vocabulary in order to advance in your job. To represent his company, your employer surely wants an employee who has not only a well-groomed physical appearance, but also a well-groomed vocabulary.

4. You may be an executive, a salesperson, lawyer, writer, teacher, administrator, preacher, or speaker

who depends daily on words, using them as tools in presenting thoughts, building arguments, being more persuasive, establishing new ideas and programs, or in being more descriptive and informative. Clearly, in this case you desire a better vocabulary so that you can do a better job.

5. You may be preparing for a college entrance examination, a civil service test, or a professional exam. Colleges routinely test the vocabulary of candidates, since a significant portion of college programs is devoted to understanding the ideas of eminent thinkers and scholars who frequently use sophisticated words. Other groups, including employers, often test an applicant's vocabulary in the belief that the size of one's vocabulary is an indicator of that person's ability and future performance.

6. You may be a concerned parent who has read reports from colleges claiming that new enrollees can neither read nor write the English language. You may have been influenced by recent television commercials urging parents to aid and encourage their children to be more studious. Thus informed, you have decided to do your part to help your college-bound youngsters become more knowledgeable about words.

Having decided to pursue a new and expanded vocabulary, you should now ask the question, "Why should I use *Big Words for Big Shooters* when a myriad of books dot the library and bookstore shelves, all professing to increase, build, improve, and add to my vocabulary in only a few free minutes a day or in a few easy lessons?" This book differs from most others in that it has been organized to help the reader improve his or her vocabulary with a minimum of time and effort:

- Lengthy exercises have been replaced by a refreshingly simple, no-nonsense approach to word learning—a quiz at the end of each chapter, for self-scoring by the reader. This approach has allowed for a larger selection of words—seven hundred, in fact—hundreds more than in the currently popular vocabulary books.
- The words in this book were selected for their frequent occurrence in newspapers, novels, magazines, television, radio, speeches, debates, commentaries, and college entrance examinations. Thus, they are useful, important, and current.
- Words with similar meanings have been grouped together.
- For simplification, only a word's most commonly used pronunciation is provided.
- Only a word's most popular and concise definition is provided.
- A preposition that commonly accompanies a word will follow it, in parentheses, in the definition.
- Each entry includes an illustration of the word used in a sentence.

Physical self-improvement programs are sweeping the country as a result of our heightened interest in jogging, dieting, and tennis and racquetball clubs. Radio and television programs, newspaper articles, books, and magazines are devoted to the topic of exercising the body and reducing it to trimness and slimness. Sadly, however, there is little emphasis on exercising the most important and exercisable part of the body—the mind. Many of us will run to feel good, dye and style our hair to look good, use carefully selected perfumes and deodorants to smell good, but do nothing to improve our reading, writing, and speaking skills. Yet what can increase the dimensions of our personalities more effectively than a new, more sophisticated vocabulary?

Truly, some magnificent and noble strangers are knocking at your brain's door. Open up and welcome these new words. As you become more acquainted with them, you will find their presence not so disturbing, their intentions not so mystifying and cryptic. Be assured that in less time than you think, they will become not only your greatest asset, but also treasured and trusted companions on whom you will rely for the rest of your life.

# Big Words for Big Shooters

1. **ephemeral** adj. (i-fem′ər-əl)
   short-lived; not lasting; transitory
   adv. ephemerally
   noun ephemera
   All of us enjoy the ephemeral beauty of
   autumn.

2. **transitory** adj. (tran′sə-tôr′ē)
   short-lived; not lasting; transient
   adv. transitorily
   noun transitoriness
   Suburban populations are often transitory.

3. **transient** adj. (tran′shənt)
   short-lived; not lasting; temporary
      adv. transiently
      noun transient—a person or thing that is
                          transient
      noun transientness
      noun transiency
      noun transcience
         The gift shop caters to a transient tourist
         trade.

4. **evanescent** adj. (ev′ə-nəs′ənt)
   short-lived; not lasting; vanishing
      adv. evanescently
      noun evanescene
      verb evanesce
         Evanescent rays of sunshine poked through
         the trees of the forest.

5. **benign** adj. (bi-nīn′)
   gentle; kind; favorable
      adj. benignant (bi-nig′nənt)
      adv. benignly
      adv. benignantly
      noun benignancy
      noun benignity—a good deed; a favor
         The benign disposition of Santa Claus
         attracts children.

6. **glabrous** adj. (glā'brəs)
   bald
   > A glabrous head gathers no dandruff.

7. **altruistic** adj. (al'trōō-is'tik)
   concerned about the well-being of others;
   benevolent
   > adv. altruistically
   > noun altruism
   > noun altruist
   >> Ministers are associated with altruistic
   >> characteristics.

8. **benevolent** adj. (bə-nev'ə-lənt)
   inclined to do good; charitable
   > adv. benevolently
   > noun benevolence
   >> A benevolent man gave the panhandler
   >> (beggar) fifty cents for a hot bowl of soup.

9. **amicable** adj. (am'i-kə-bəl)
   friendly
   > adv. amicably
   > noun amicability
   > noun amicableness
   >> The couple agreed to an amicable separa-
   >> tion.

10. **amiable** adj. (ā′mē-ə-bəl)
    friendly; kindhearted
       adv. amiably
       noun amiability
       noun amiableness
          It was just an amiable basketball game between old friends.


11. **beneficent** adj. (bə-nef′ə-sənt)
    doing good; acting kindly
       adj. benefic
       adv. beneficently
       noun beneficence
          The beneficent king had many loyal and happy subjects.


12. **chivalrous** adj. (shiv′əl-rəs)
    gallant; generous; courteous
       adj. chivalric
       adv. chivalrously
       noun chivalrousness
       noun chivalry
          Gentlemen are expected to be chivalrous.


13. **palfrey** noun (pôl′frē)
    a horse
          A gainly (graceful) two-year-old palfrey won the furturity.

14. **malign** adj. (mə-līn′)
    hateful; evil in nature
    adj. malignant (mə-lig′nənt)
    adv. malignly
    adv. malignantly
    noun malignancy
    noun malignance
    noun malignity
    noun maligner
    verb malign—to slander, to defame
    The malign disposition of Dracula scares
    many children.

15. **vilify** verb (vil′ə-fī)
    to speak evil of; to slander; to malign
    noun vilifier
    noun vilification
    Threats to vilify him in public had no effect.

16. **maleficent** adj. (mə-lef′ə-sənt)
    doing harm; acting evilly
    adj. malefic
    noun maleficence
    The maleficent king had many disloyal and
    unhappy subjects.

17. **euphemism** noun (yoo′fe-miz′əm)
    a mild word or expression
    adj. euphemistic
    adj. euphemistical
    adv. euphemistically
    noun euphemist—one who uses euphemisms
    verb euphemize
    Sanitary engineer is a euphemism for
    janitor.

18. **bibliophile** noun (bib′lē-ə-fīl′)
    a lover of books
    adj. bibliophilistic
    noun bibliophilist
    noun bibliophilism
    The bibliophile spent all his free time at the library.

19. **holograph** adj. (hol′ə-graf)
    written by person whose signature it bears
    adj. holographic
    adj. holographical
    noun holograph
    Receiving a holograph letter from the kidnapped man renewed hopes.

20. **calligraphy** noun (kə-lig′rə-fē)
    a beautiful handwriting; penmanship in general
    adj. calligraphic
    noun calligrapher
    noun calligraphist
    The calligraphy of the priests who wrote Bibles during the Middle Ages was beautiful.

21. **lexicon** noun (lek′sə-kon)
    a dictionary
    adj. lexicographic
    adj. lexicographical
    adv. lexicographically
    noun lexicography—the practice of writing dictionaries
    noun lexicographer—a writer of dictionaries
    All students should possess a lexicon.

22. **lexical** adj. (lek′sə-kəl)
    pertaining to words
    > Because of his impressive vocabulary, he
    > was called a lexical wizard.

23. **peruse** verb (pə-rōōz′)
    to read carefully
    adj. perusable
    noun perusal—the act of reading carefully
    noun peruser
    > The teacher asked the class to peruse the
    > complex chapter.

24. **relative** adj. (rel′ə-tiv)
    relating to; in regards to; pertinent to
    adv. relatively
    noun relativeness
    > The doctor made an inquiry relative to the
    > patient's health.

25. **obdurate** adj. (ob′dyə-rit)
    unyielding; hardened against persuasions;
    inexorable
    adv. obdurately
    noun obduracy
    noun obdurateness
    > He remained obdurate despite the pres-
    > sure.

26. **inexorable** adj. (in-ek′sər-ə-bəl)
    unyielding; relentless
    adv. inexorably
    noun inexorability
    noun inexorableness
        The inexorable bill collector would not compromise.

27. **adamant** adj. (ad′ə-mant)
    unyielding; hardened against persuasions; inexorable; impenetrable
        The politician took an adamant position against amnesty for detractors.

28. **vehement** adj. (vē′ə-mənt)
    eager; forceful; energetic; ardent
    adv. vehemently
    noun vehemence
    noun vehemency
        A vehement dislike for the proposal was expressed by the majority.

29. **resolute** adj. (rez′ə-lo͞ot)
    determined; steady; set in purpose
    adv. resolutely
    noun resoluteness
    noun resolution—a determination; a firmness of purpose
        The mayor reiterated that he was resolute in not seeking another term.

30. **ardent** adj. (är′dənt)
passionate; zealous; intense; vehement
adv. ardently
noun ardentness
noun ardency
noun ardor
Are you an ardent patriot?

31. **fervent** adj. (fûr′vənt)
ardent; enthusiastic; showing great warmth
adv. fervently
noun ferventness
noun fervency
The fervent little dog greeted its master at
the door.

32. **sedulous** adj. (sej′ŏo-ləs)
persevering; diligent; devoted
adv. sedulously
noun sedulousness
Sedulous workers are a company's
greatest asset.

33. **zealous** adj. (zel′əs)
devoted; eager; ardent; diligent; energetic
adv. zealously
noun zealousness
noun zealotry
noun zealot
noun zeal
The zealous beagle ran a rabbit for
several hours.

34. **assiduous** adj. (ə-sij′ōō-əs)
   eager; devoted; diligent
   adv. assiduously
   noun assiduousness
   noun assiduity (as′ə-dōō′ə-tē)
   Assiduous study is a prerequisite for good grades.

35. **strenuous** adj. (stren′yōō-əs)
   1. eager; ardent; energetic; diligent
   2. requiring great exertion
   adv. strenuously
   noun strenuousity
   noun strenuousness
   The candidate proved to be a strenuous opponent.

36. **arduous** adj. (är′jōō-əs)
   difficult; laborious; requiring much labor
   adv. arduously
   noun arduousness
   Despite an arduous effort, he failed.

37. **laborious** adj. (lə-bôr′ē-əs)
   difficult; arduous; requiring much labor
   adv. laboriously
   noun laboriousness
   The laborious building of the Egyptian pyramids astonishes (amazes) everyone.

38. **onerous** adj. (on′ər-əs)
    burdensome; troublesome; requiring much labor
    adv. onerously
    noun onerousness
      The chain gang began the onerous task of
      cracking rocks with sledge hammers.


39. **celestial** adj. (sə-les′chəl)
    pertaining to the sky; heavenly divine
    adv. celestially
      Under a bright celestial sky, the shepherd
      stood watching over his flock.


40. **befuddle** verb (bi-fud′l)
    to confuse
      Alcohol is known to befuddle the reasoning
      process.


41. **obfuscate** verb (ob-fus′kāt)
    to confuse
    noun obfuscation
      The neophyte (beginner) debater will more
      than likely obfuscate the basic issues.


42. **enigmatic** adj. (en′ig-mat′ik)
    puzzling; mysterious; baffling
    adj. enigmatical
    adv. enigmatically
    noun enigma—a puzzle, a confusing problem
      The police found many enigmatic events
      surrounding the homicide.

43. **hedonist** noun (hēd′n-ist)
    one who pursues pleasures as the chief aim in life; a pleasure-seeker
    adj. hedonic
    adj. hedonistic
    adv. hedonically
    adv. hedonistically
    noun hedonism
    noun hedonics
    > The hedonist claimed work was contrary to his life style.

44. **harbinger** noun (här′bin-jər)
    a forerunner
    > The swallow is a harbinger of spring.

45. **precursor** noun (pri-kûr′sər)
    a forerunner
    adj. precursory—preliminary
    adj. precursive—preliminary
    > The scout was the precursor of an entire army regiment.

46. **advent** noun (ad′vent)
    an arrival
    > The advent of computors has facilitated (made easy) intricate computations.

47. **dire** adj. (dīr)
    dreadful; awful; terrible
       adj. direful
       adj. direr
       adj. direst
       adv. direly
       adv. direfully
       noun direfulness
       noun direness
          The hunter was lost and in dire need of
          food.

48. **celerity** noun (sə-ler′ə-tē)
    speed; quickness
          The celerity of the delivery was unequaled.

49. **alacrity** noun (ə-lak′ra-tē)
    liveliness; cheerful eagerness; briskness
       adj. alacritous
          Regardless of the weather the mailman de-
          livered letters with alacrity.

50. **expeditious** adj. (ek′spə-dish′əs)
    speedy; quick
       adv. expeditiously
       noun expeditiousness
       noun expediter
       verb expedite—to speed up
          Construction of the home was expeditious,
          yet meticulous (careful attention to detail).

51. **abstemious** adj. (ab-stē′mē-əs)
    moderate in eating and drinking
    adv. abstemiously
    noun abstemiousness
    By no means is fat Fanny abstemious.


52. **expedient** adj. (ik-spē′dē-ənt)
    advantageous; advisable
    adj. expediential—(ik-spē′dē-en′shəl)
    adv. expediently
    noun expediency
    noun expedience
    She thought it expedient to conceal her
    past employment record.


53. **vitiated** adj. (vish′ē-ā′tid)
    contaminated; corrupted; spoiled
    adj. vitiable
    noun vitiation
    noun vitiator
    verb vitiate—to corrupt or spoil

    Benign (kind) deeds are occasionally vi-
    tiated motives in disguise.


54. **vivacious** adj. (vi-vā′shəs)
    lively; full of life; active
    adv. vivaciously
    noun vivaciousness
    noun vivacity
    The vivacious conversation drew a crowd.

55. **effervescent** adj. (ef'ər-ves'ənt)
   sparkling; lively; gay; vivacious
   noun effervescence
   noun effervescency
   verb effervesce—to show liveliness
   The employer claimed effervescent secretaries were his type.


56. **jaunty** adj. (jôn'tē)
   cheerful and lively
   adv. jauntily
   noun jauntiness
   He walked with jaunty steps after winning the lottery.


57. **vibrant** adj. (vī'brənt)
   energetic; full of vigor; throbbing
   adv. vibrantly
   noun vibrancy
   Red is considered a vibrant color.


58. **scintillating** adj. (sin'tə-lāt'ing)
   sparkling; flashing
   adj. scintillant
   adv. scintillatingly
   noun scintillation
   verb scintillate
   His scintillating wit kept everybody amused.

59. **titillate** verb (tit′ə-lāt)

to tickle; to excite in a pleasurable way
adj. titillative
noun titillation
noun titillant—an excitant
The professor told the class he hoped to enlighten their minds, not titillate their fancies.

60. **sanguine** adj. (sang′gwin)

cheerful; confident; hopeful
adv. sanguinely
noun sanguineness
People with sanguine dispositions are pleasant company.

61. **convivial** adj. (kən-viv′ē-əl)

sociable; jovial; festive
adv. convivially
noun conviviality
noun convivialist
Holidays involve the convivial company of friends and relatives.

62. **gregarious** adj. (gri-gâr′ē-əs)

sociable; crowd loving
adv. gregariously
noun gregariousness
Sheep are gregarious animals.

63. **felicity** noun (fə-lis′ə-tē)
    happiness; bliss
        adj. felicific—(fē′lə-sif′ik)—producing happi-
                ness
        He was eagerly looking forward to the
        felicity of retirement.


64. **felicitation** noun (fə-lis′ə-tā′shən)
    congratulation
        verb felicitate—to congratulate
        The sweepstakes winner received cards of
        felicitation from all over the country.


65. **felicitous** adj. (fə-lis′ə-təs)
    appropriate; apt
        adv. felicitously
        noun felicitousness
        His felicitous remarks made him a great
        master of ceremonies.


66. **apropos** adj. (ap′rə-pō′)
    pertinent; apt; suitable
        The economist made apropos remarks on
        the state of the economy.


67. **congenial** adj. (kən-jēn′yəl)
    agreeable
        adv. congenially
        noun congeniality—(kən-jē′nē-al′ə-tē)
        They enjoy a congenial companionship.


27

68. **reconcile** verb (rek′ən-sĭl)
    to bring into harmony; to settle
      adj. reconcilable—able to be reconciled
      adj. reconciliatory—tending to reconcile
      adv. reconcilably
      noun reconcilability
      noun reconcilableness
      noun reconcilement
      noun reconciler
        Friends hope the couple will be able to reconcile their differences before the children are affected.


69. **vigilant** adj. (vij′ə-lənt)
    watchful; alert
      adv. vigilantly
      noun vigilantness
      noun vigilance
        The security guard is more vigilant than any they've had before.


70. **despair** noun (di-spâr′)
    hopelessness
      adj. despairing
      adv. despairingly
      noun despairingness
      verb despair—to lose hope
        There he sits upon a chair,
        in a state of deep despair,
        because he lost all his hair.

71. **desolate** adj. (des′ə-lit)
    1. barren; uninhabited; deserted
    2. sad; gloomy
    3. lonely
       adv. desolately
       noun desolaterer
       noun desolator
       noun desolateness
       noun desolation
       verb—desolate—(des′ə-lāt)—to make sorrowful; to devastate
    Being alone on a desolate island may be very depressing.

72. **disconsolate** adj. (dis-kon′sə-lit)
    gloomy; saturnine; dejected
       adv. disconsolately
       noun disconsolation
       noun disconsolateness
    A disconsolate atmosphere prevailed in the locker room after the game was lost.

73. **saturnine** adj. (sat′ər-nīn)
    gloomy; morose
    A good joke can erase a saturnine facial expression.

74. **morose** adj. (mə-rōs′)
    gloomy; sullen
       adv. morosely
       noun moroseness
    Falling stock prices create morose stockbrokers.

75. **doleful** adj. (dōl'fəl)
   gloomy; melancholy
      adv. dolefully
      noun dolefulness
         He has the doleful look of a man possessed
         with difficulties.

76. **melancholy** adj. (mel'ən-kol'ē)
   extremely gloomy; despondent
      adj. melancholic
      adv. melanchollically
      noun melancholia—a mental disorder caused
                        by deep depression
      noun melancholiac—one affected with gloom
         A change of environment is good for a
         melancholy disposition.

77. **despondent** adj. (di-spon'dənt)
   gloomy; dejected
      adv. despondently
      adv. despondingly
      noun despondence
      noun despondency
      verb despond—to lose hope or spirit
         The despondent family sat together at the
         funeral.

78. **lugubrious** adj. (lōō-gōō'brē-əs)
   very sad; dismal
      adv. lugubriously
      noun lugubriousness
         The basset hound's face is more lugubrious
         than a beagle's.

79. **lachrymose** adj. (lak′rə-mōs)
    causing tears; sad; tearful
      adj. lachrymatory
      adj. lachrymal
      adj. lacrimal
      adj. lacrymal
      adv. lachrymosely
        The lachrymose story of Bambi was made
        into a movie.


80. **soporific** adj. (sop′ə-rif′ik)
    causing sleep; drowsy; sleepy; lethargic
      adj. soporiferous
      adv. soporiferously
      noun soporiferousness
        An overdose of soporific drugs, if not
        fatal, may lead to severe complications.


81. **lethargic** adj. (li-thär′jik)
    excessively drowsy; sleepy; listless; apathetic
      adj. lethargical
      adv. lethargically
      noun lethargy
      verb lethargize—to make drowsy
        A lethargic feeling overcame him after
        going without sleep three nights in a row.


82. **lassitude** noun (las′ə-tōōd)
    a state of fatigue; languidness
        After a weekend of skiing, he suffered from
        lassitude.

83. **languid** adj. (lang′gwid)
    1. affected by weakness; drowsy due to fatigue
    2. indifferent; lacking spirit
       adv. languidly
       noun languidness
           With languid effort, the marathon dancer
           removed his shoes.

84. **languorous** adj. (lang′gər-əs)
    1. drowsy; due to dreaminess
    2. dull; inactive
       adv. languorously
       noun languorousness
       noun languor—listlessness
           He spent a languorous afternoon swinging
           in a hammock.

85. **lackadaisical** adj. (lak′ə-dā′zi-kəl)
    lack of energy or interest; lack of concern; list-
    less; uninterested
       adv. lackadaisically
       noun lackadaisicalness
           Having jogged for two-hours, he was com-
           pletely lackadaisical about playing tennis.

86. **feckless** adj. (fek′lis)
    1. devoid of energy; listless
    2. careless; not responsible
       adv. fecklessly
       noun fecklessness
           Only a feckless attempt was made to weed
           the garden.

87. **debilitate** verb (di-bil′ə-tāt)
     to weaken
          adj. debilitative
          noun debilitation
          noun debility—feebleness
          Sickness will debilitate one's body.

88. **enervate** verb (en′ər-vāt)
     to weaken
          adj. enervate (i-nûr′vit)—weakened; lacking
                                        energy
          noun enervation
          noun enervator
          Exposure to an extremely hot sun will
          enervate the body to the point of collapse.

89. **giddy** adj. (gid′ē)
     flighty; light headed; impulsive; dizzy
          adj. giddier—dizzier
          adj. giddiest—dizziest
          adv. giddily
          noun giddiness
          Don't try to figure out that giddy dame's
          next move.

90. **impulsive** adj. (im-pul′siv)
     acting without forethought; spontaneous
          adv. impulsively
          noun impulsiveness
          noun impulsion
          noun impulse
          The impulsive child darted into the street,
          chasing a misdirected ball.

91. **impetuous** adj. (im-pech′ōō-əs)
    acting without forethought; recklessly hasty
    adv. impetuously
    noun impetuousness
    noun impetuousity
    > More impetuous pilots are in the ground than in the air.

92. **fickle** adj. (fik′əl)
    changeable; wavering; capricious
    noun fickleness
    > Because of her fickle nature, we never knew if she was coming or going.

93. **willynilly** adj. (wil′ē nil′ē)
    uncertain; indecisive; wavering; fluctuating
    > When fickle Nilly and capricious Willy got married, they created a willynilly partnership.

94. **capricious** adj. (kə-prish′əs)
    fickle; shifting; inclined to change quickly
    adv. capriciously
    noun capriciousness
    noun caprice
    > Because she is capricious, her actions are facetious (humorous).

95. **mutable** adj. (myoo'tə-bəl)
    1. capable of change; alterable; subject to change,
    2. fickle
       adv. mutably
       noun mutableness
       noun mutability
       Our club has expressed a mutable desire to have a picnic on that date.

96. **arbitrary** adj. (är'bə-trer'ē)
    capricious; subject to individual whim, will or judgement
       adv. arbitrarily
       noun arbitrariness
       An arbitrary interpretation of such an important plan cannot be tolerated.

97. **quaff** verb (kwof) or (kwaf)
    to drink deeply and abundantly
       noun quaff—a drink or a swallow
       noun quaffer
       Big Mike could quaff a pitcher of brew without taking a breath.

98. **amenable** adj. (ə-men'ə-bəl)
    capable of being persuaded; submissive
       adv. amenably
       noun amenability
       noun amenableness
       All the residents were amenable to the new crime-fighting legislation.

99. **acquiescent** adj. (ak′wē-es′ənt)
yielding; submissive; agreeable
adv. acquiescently
adv. acquiescingly
noun acquiescence
verb acquiesce—to yield (use with the word
in)
We will follow your suggestion, as we
are quite acquiescent.

100. **tractable** adj. (trak′tə-bəl)
manageable; easily controlled; docile
adv. tractably
noun tractableness
noun tractability
Amigo is unusually tractable for a donkey.

## Test 1

1. abstemious a. biological b. moderate c. eager
   d. difficult
2. acquiescent a. yielding b. understanding
   c. coarse d. audible
3. adamant a. sharp b. profound c. harmonious
   d. unyielding
4. advent a. arrival b. adventure c. agreement
   d. default
5. alacrity a. briskness b. seriousness
   c. violation d. transition
6. altruistic a. truthful b. carefree c. lively
   d. benevolent
7. amenable a. bold b. remarkable c. submissive
   d. harmless
8. amiable a. honest b. flamboyant c. unknown
   d. kindhearted
9. amicable a. uninformed b. perfect
   c. unenjoyable d. friendly
10. apropos a. proportionate b. apt c. automatic
    d. fictitious
11. arbitrary a. ambitious b. devoted c. steady
    d. capricious
12. ardent a. exhilarating b. lazy c. impossible
    d. zealous
13. arduous a. difficult b. blissful c. atrocious
    d. sarcastic
14. assiduous a. treacherous b. diligent
    c. rebellious d. helpful
15. befuddle a. confuse b. swindle c. obligate
    d. appreciate
16. beneficent a. doing good b. well-made
    c. sociable d. sensitive

17. benevolent  a. genuine  b. charitable  c. violent
    d. insulting
18. benign  a. soft  b. clever  c. unstable  d. gentle
19. bibliophile  a. book container  b. librarian
    c. book lover  d. language professor
20. calligraphy  a. worthless nicknacks
    b. paraphernalia  c. penmanship  d. collection
21. capricious  a. timely  b. shy  c. fickle  d. stingy
22. celerity  a. exception  b. quickness  c. criticism
    d. hardship
23. celestial  a. heavenly  b. rustic  c. murky
    d. selfish
24. chivalrous  a. faultfinding  b. courteous
    c. harmonious  d. frigid
25. congenial  a. disinterested  b. agreeable
    c. ordinary  d. useless
26. convivial  a. shrewd  b. sociable  c. occasional
    d. loving
27. debilitate  a. put off  b. trick  c. repel  d. weaken
28. desolate  a. barren  b. unemotional  c. harsh
    d. unknown
29. despair  a. shabbiness  b. disorder  c. decadence
    d. hopelessness
30. despondent  a. gloomy  b. slow  c. calm
    d. sickly
31. dire  a. unavoidable  b. awful  c. mean and ugly
    d. fearful
32. disconsolate  a. exhausted  b. threatening
    c. gloomy  d. loose
33. doleful  a. tedious  b. peaceful  c. poisonous
    d. melancholy
34. effervescent  a. enjoyable  b. short-lived
    c. variable  d. lively

35. enervate  a. steal  b. decide  c. weaken  d. liven
36. enigmatic  a. dangerous  b. puzzling
    c. destructive  d. inspiring
37. ephemeral  a. transitory  b. immortal
    c. unusual  d. concise
38. euphemism  a. imitation  b. mild word
    c. transitoriness  d. praise
39. evanescent  a. mysterious  b. vanishing
    c. religious  d. lively
40. expedient  a. advantageous  b. fast
    c. enlightening  d. necessary
41. expeditious  a. worthy  b. obscure  c. profound
    d. speedy
42. feckless  a. listless  b. not typical  c. foolish
    d. spotted
43. felicitation  a. sad feeling  b. exposure
    c. congratulation  d. happiness
44. felicitous  a. catlike  b. happy  c. appropriate
    d. poor
45. felicity  a. happiness  b. eagerness  c. sleeping
    d. advice
46. fervent  a. involuntary  b. thrifty  c. fierce
    d. enthusiastic
47. fickle  a. debatable  b. changeable  c. showy
    d. reasonable
48. giddy  a. flighty  b. disabled  c. indifferent
    d. fastidious
49. glabrous  a. swollen  b. brilliant  c. flabby
    d. bald
50. gregarious  a. helpful  b. worthless  c. playful
    d. sociable
51. harbinger  a. bird  b. fertility  c. worshiper
    d. forerunner

52. hedonist  a. wicked witch  b. sadistic person
    c. lover of books  d. pleasure seeker
53. holograph  a. printed letter  b. wired message
    c. hand written work  d. telephone recording
54. impetuous  a. ungrateful  b. lenient
    c. recklessly hasty  d. unsuited
55. impulsive  a. notorious  b. naive
    c. spontaneous  d. indigent
56. inexorable  a. insulting  b. horrible
    c. unyeilding  d. sparkling
57. jaunty  a. cheerful  b. popular  c. graceful
    d. absurd
58. laborious  a. casual  b. sorrowful  c. stylish
    d. difficult
59. lachrymose  a. causing excitement  b. humble
    c. causing tears  d. heavy
60. lackadaisical  a. dizzy  b. unconcerned
    c. modest  d. lacking
61. languid  a. drowsy  b. lionlike  c. greedy
    d. incompatible
62. languorous a. loathsome  b. sacred  c. inactive
    d. piercing
63. lassitude  a. state of excitement
    b. replacement  c. state of fatigue  d. despair
64. lethargic  a. sleepless  b. informal  c. dull
    d. awkward
65. lexical  a. elfin b. related to words
    c. many sided d. tough
66. lexicon  a. dictionary  b. little person
    c. criminal  d. intruder
67. lugubrious  a. very sad  b. handsome
    c. ridiculous  d. inexperienced

68. maleficient  a. gradual  b. doing harm
    c. mournful  d. strenuous
69. malign  a. out of line  b. hateful  c. corrective
    d. sloppy
70. melancholy  a. gloomy  b. smooth  c. soothing
    d. hot-tempered
71. morose  a. stupid  b. brief  c. flashy  d. sullen
72. mutable  a. quiet  b. muffled  c. stubborn
    d. alterable
73. obdurate  a. pleasurable  b. protective
    c. inexorable  d. subtle
74. obfuscate  a. make excuses  b. confuse
    c. confront  d. clear of charges
75. onerous  a. burdensome  b. knowing all things
    c. malicious  d. gentle
76. palfrey  a. baby fish  b. horse
    c. casket covering  d. outcast
77. peruse  a. perform  b. to exhaust the supply
    c. crawl  d. to read carefully
78. precursor  a. harbinger  b. investigator
    c. hermit  d. miser
79. quaff  a. to shout loudly  b. drink
    c. exterminate  d. think
80. reconcile  a. to make saleable  b. surrender
    c. bring into harmony  d. steal
81. relative  a. friendly  b. reciprocal  c. mutual
    d. relating to
82. resolute  a. wordy  b. radiant  c. tired
    d. determined
83. sanguine  a. rough  b. winterly  c. cowardly
    d. hopeful
84. saturnine  a. heavenly  b. gloomy  c. secretive
    d. improper

85. scintillating a. sparkling b. exciting
c. amusing d. foolish
86. sedulous a. diligent b. profane c. abundant
d. ludicrous
87. soporific a. saturated b. causing sleep
c. tireless d. desirable
88. strenuous a. requiring great exertion
b. worthy of reward c. dishonest
d. ill-smelling
89. titillate a. repulse b. intensify c. excite
d. spread
90. tractable a. uncontrollable b. manageable
c. slippery d. powerful
91. transient a. temporary b. rash c. permanent
d. unconquerable
92. transitory a. not lasting b. commendable
c. inaccurate d. clear
93. vehement a. disorderly b. cruel c. eager
d. quarrelsome
94. vibrant a. colorful b. noisy c. aimless
d. energetic
95. vigilant a. customary b. worried
c. faultfinding d. watchful
96. vilify a. praise b. kill c. slander d. trick
97. vitiated a. full of life b. idle c. spoiled
d. earnest
98. vivacious a. tasty b. charming c. lively
d. entertaining
99. willynilly a. idiotic b. unskilled c. uncertain
d. disliked
100. zealous a. incorrect b. energetic c. sluggish
d. rapid

# Test 1
## Answers

| | | | |
|---|---|---|---|
| 1. b | 26. b | 51. d | 76. b |
| 2. a | 27. d | 52. d | 77. d |
| 3. d | 28. a | 53. c | 78. a |
| 4. a | 29. d | 54. c | 79. b |
| 5. a | 30. a | 55. c | 80. c |
| 6. d | 31. b | 56. c | 81. d |
| 7. c | 32. c | 57. a | 82. d |
| 8. d | 33. d | 58. d | 83. d |
| 9. d | 34. d | 59. c | 84. b |
| 10. b | 35. c | 60. b | 85. a |
| 11. d | 36. b | 61. a | 86. a |
| 12. d | 37. a | 62. c | 87. b |
| 13. a | 38. b | 63. c | 88. a |
| 14. b | 39. b | 64. c | 89. c |
| 15. a | 40. a | 65. b | 90. b |
| 16. a | 41. d | 66. a | 91. a |
| 17. b | 42. a | 67. a | 92. a |
| 18. d | 43. c | 68. b | 93. c |
| 19. c | 44. c | 69. b | 94. d |
| 20. c | 45. a | 70. a | 95. d |
| 21. c | 46. d | 71. d | 96. c |
| 22. b | 47. b | 72. d | 97. c |
| 23. a | 48. a | 73. c | 98. c |
| 24. b | 49. d | 74. b | 99. c |
| 25. b | 50. d | 75. a | 100. b |

## SCORING

Correct answers
- 100-90 = A (excellent)
- 89-80 = B (good)
- 79-70 = C (fair)
- 69-60 = D (poor)
- 59- 0 = E (Start over!)

Score before word study _____

Score after word study _____

101. **accede** verb (ak-sēd′)

    to agree; to consent (used with the word to)
    noun accedence
    noun acceder
        Please don't accede to such an absurd plan.

102. **apparition** noun (ap′ə-rish′ən)

    a ghost
      adj. apparitional
        Townspeople claimed the house was
        haunted by an apparition of the man mur-
        dered there years ago.

103. **derelict** adj. (der′ə-likt)

    neglectful
      noun derelict—something abandoned; one
               who is negligent; a social
               outcast
      noun dereliction
        Derelict attention resulted in a confusing
        bank book.

104. **pretermit** verb (prē′tər-mit′)

    to disregard; to neglect; to omit; to overlook
    noun pretermission
    noun pretermitter
        The coach may pretermit a mistake once,
        but never twice.

105. **inadvertent** adj. (in′əd-vûr′tənt)
    negligent; oversight; unintentional
        adv. inadvertently
        noun inadvertence
        noun inadvertency
            The flooded basement was caused by the
            inadvertent act of not turning off a faucet.


106. **fortuitous** adj. (fôr-tōō′ə-təs)
    accidental
        adv. fortuitously
        noun fortuitousness
        noun fortuity—an accidental happening
            The couple met under fortuitous cir-
            cumstances.


107. **adventitious** adj. (ad′ven-tish′əs)
    accidental; casual
        adv. adventitiously
        noun adventitiousness
            Success is not an adventitious occurrence;
            you must roll up your sleeves and work
            hard.


108. **latent** adj. (lā′tənt)
    concealed; not visible or apparent
        adv. latently
        noun latency—the state of being concealed
            The employee suggested latent dissatisfac-
            tions exist in the department over recent
            promotions.

109. **covert** adj. (kō′vərt)
concealed; secret; hidden
adv. covertly
noun covertness
The special agents arranged a covert meeting place.

110. **clandestine** adj. (klan-dĕs′tin)
secret; sly
adv. clandestinely
noun clandestineness
A clandestine plan exists to overthrow the regime.

111. **surreptitious** adj. (sûr′əp-tish′əs)
secret; sly
adv. surreptitiously
noun surreptitiousness
Surreptitious agents will infiltrate the regime.

112. **furtive** adj. (fûr′tiv)
secret; sly
adv. furtively
noun furtiveness
She gave a furtive glance in his direction.

113. **patent** adj. (pat′nt)
obvious; apparent
adj. patentable
adv. patently
noun patency
noun patentability
Crime is a patent problem in most large cities.

114. **palpable** adj. (pal′pǝ-bǝl)
    obvious; apparent
      adv. palpably
      noun palpability
      noun palpableness
        Sunshine, blossoming flowers and green-ery are palpable signs of spring.

115. **ostensible** adj. (os-ten′sǝ-bǝl)
    apparent; genuine
      adv. ostensibly
        The extremely low price on the vacuum sweeper was an ostensible mistake, not a deceitful ploy (maneuver) to sell sweepers.

116. **ostensive** adj. (os-ten′siv)
    apparent
      adv. ostensively
        An ostensive movement exists to discourage his entry.

117. **salient** adj. (sā′lē-ǝnt)
    conspicuous; noticeable
      adv. saliently
      noun salience
      noun saliency
      noun salientness
        One of the salient features of that car is its winged rear fenders.

118. **eminent** adj. (em′ə-nənt)
     distinguished; prominent; superior; outstanding
     adv. eminently
     noun eminency
     noun eminence
        The assembly heard remarks by an eminent scholar.

119. **imminent** adj. (im′ə-nənt)
     close; about to happen
     adv. imminently
     noun imminency
     noun imminence
        Fearing imminent aerial attacks, the inhabitants fled their village.

120. **inchoate** adj. (in-kō′it)
     beginning; early stage; incipient; not complete
     adj. inchoative (in-kō′ə-tiv)
     adv. inchoately
     noun inchoateness
     noun inchoation
        The civic center is in the inchoate stages of construction planning.

121. **incipient** adj. (in-sip′ē-ənt)
     beginning; early stage; inchoate
     adv. incipiently
     noun incipience
     noun incipiency
        The flower was picked at its incipient stage of bloom.

122. **moor** verb (mŏŏr)
     to secure
          Don't moor your boat at private docks.

123. **conflagration** noun (kon'fla-grā'shǝn)
     a large fire
          adj. conflagrant—burning fiercely
          The conflagration destroyed acres of prime
          timber.

124. **holocaust** noun (hol'ǝ-kôst)
     destruction (usually by fire)
          adj. holocaustal
          adj. holocaustic
          All large cities fear holocaust.

125. **anomalous** adj. (ǝ-nom'ǝ-lǝs)
     abnormal; irregular
          adj. anomalistic
          adj. anomalistical
          adv. anomalously
          noun anomalousness
          noun anomaly
          noun anomalism
          It would be anomalous to see Red, the
          rooster, up after sunset.

126. **aberrant** adj. (ab-er'ǝnt)
     abnormal; wandering; varying
          noun aberrance
          noun aberration
          noun aberrancy
          Thermometers are commonly aberrant
          in early spring.

127. **vacillating** adj. (vas'ə-lā'ting)
   wavering; fluctuating
   adj. vacillatory
   adj. vacillant
   adv. vacillatingly
   noun vacillancy
   noun vacillation
   verb vacillate
   The vacillating stock market has probably
   produced more ulcers than millionaires.

128. **errant** adj. (er'rənt)
   1. wandering; itinerant
   2. straying from correct standard
   adv. errantly
   Errant gypsies are of oriental origin.

129. **itinerant** adj. (ī-tin'ər-ənt)
   wandering; traveling
   adv. itinerantly
   noun itinerary—a travel plan
   noun itinerancy
   noun itineracy
   noun itineration
   noun itinerant—a traveler
   verb itinerate
   The itinerant peddler had many friends.

130. **ratable** adj. (rā′tə-bəl)
   proportional
      adv. ratably
      noun ratability
      noun ratableness
         The center makes ratable distributions of
         food to the poor based on income.

131. **commensurate** adj. (kə-men′shə-rit)
   proportional
      adj. commensurable
      adv. commensurately
      adv. commensurably
      noun commensurateness
      noun commensuration
      noun commensurability
         His horrendous (horrible) display of anger
         was not commensurate with the trivialness
         of the offense.

132. **forgo** verb (fôr-gō′)
   to give up; to go without
      noun forgoer
         Sorry, but I must forgo the pleasure of
         dessert as I am on a diet.

133. **facade** noun (fə-säd)
   1. face of a building
   2. false front designed to give a favorable im-
      pression
         The facade of the building was ornately
         (elaborately) finished.

134. **numismatist** noun (noo miz′ mə-tist)
    a coin collector
      adj. numismatic
      adj. numismatical
      noun numismatics—the study of coins
      noun numismatology
      noun numismatologist
        The numismatist was grief-stricken when his collection fell prey to a burglar.

135. **philatelist** noun (fi-lat′ə-list)
    a stamp collector
      adj. philatelic
      adj. philatelical
      adv. philatelically
      noun philately—the study of stamps
        The philatelist had more money invested in his collection than he did in his home.

136. **discophile** noun (dis′kə-fīl)
    a collector of phonograph recordings
        The neighbor, a discophile, has a collection worth thousands of dollars.

137. **conjoin** verb (kən-join′)
    to join together; to unite
      adj. conjoint
      adv. conjointly
      noun conjoiner
        The new homeowners decided to conjoin and to sue the builder.

138. **concerted** adj. (kən-sûr′tid)
    done together; combined
        adv. concertedly
        noun concert—harmony; co-operation
        verb concert—to act together
            The concerted effort to rehabilitate the area succeeded.


139. **intemperate** adj. (in-tem′pər-it)
    overindulgence, excessive
        adv. intemperately
        noun intemperateness
        noun intemperance
            Intemperate indulgences should be checked.


140. **inordinate** adj. (in-ôr′də-nit)
    excessive
        adj. inordinacy
        adv. inordinately
        noun inordinacy
        noun inordinateness
            The enemy made inordinate demands.


141. **immoderate** adj. (i-mod′ər-it)
    excessive
        adv. immoderately
        noun immoderateness
            Immoderate drinkers of alcohol should never drive.

142. **in perpetuum** adv. (in-pər-pech′oo-əm)
>   forever
>> As far as the city is concerned, the tree can remain there in perpetuum, but the land-owner wants it removed immediately.

143. **bombastic** adj. (bom-bas′tik)
>   showy and exaggerated, especially relative to speech and writing
>   adj. bombastical
>   adv. bombastically
>   noun bombast
>> Car salesmen are known for their bombastic promotional speeches.

144. **pompous** adj. (pom′pəs)
>   lofty; exaggerated; splendid; showy
>   adv. pompously
>   noun pompousness
>   noun pomposity
>   noun pomp
>> The wrestler strutted around the ring in a pompous fashion.

145. **grandiose** adj. (gran′dē-ōs)
>   magnificent; impressive; pompous
>   adv. grandiosely
>   noun grandiosity
>> Audiences were more interested in his grandiose gestures than in the context of his speeches.

146. **ostentatious** adj. (os'tən-tā'shəs)
    showy
       adv. ostentatiously
       noun ostentatiousness
       noun ostentation
          Her ostentatious display of furs upset the
          environmentalist.

147. **pretentious** adj. (pri-ten'shəs)
    showy
       adv. pretentiously
       noun pretentiousness
          Her pretentious dress was inappropriate
          for the informal social event.

148. **rhetorical** adj. (ri-tôr'i-kəl)
    showy and stylish with little regard to meaning
    (especially relative to speech and writing);
    characterized by correctness, clearness and
    style of communication rather than content
       adv. rhetorically
       noun rhetoric
       noun rhetorician—a master of rhetoric
       noun rhetoricalness
          What was hailed as an important speech on
          the economy was, in reality, a mere rhetor-
          ical exercise.

149. **grandiloquent** adj. (gran-dil'ə-kwənt)
    showy and stylish, relative to speech
       adv. grandiloquently
       noun grandiloquence
          The statesman gave a grandiloquent
          speech.

150. **pontificate** verb (pon-tif′ə-kāt′)
to act, write or speak in a showy and stylish
manner
adj. pontifical
adv. pontifically
It wasn't his style to pontificate; instead, he
presented the information quickly and simply.


151. **sumptuous** adj. (sump′choo-əs)
costly; superb; magnificent; luxurious
adv. sumptuously
noun sumptuousness
The sumptuous mansion opens for tourism
next weekend.


152. **histrionics** noun (his′trē-on′iks)
dramatics; acting
adj. histrionic
adj. histrional
adv. histrionically
She is pursuing a histrionics career.


153. **plethoric** adj. (ple-thôr′ik)
superabundant; overfull
adv. plethorically
noun plethora—superabundance
Plethoric wild flowers mark the trail that
twists through the woods.

154. **profuse** adj. (prə-fyo͞os′)
    abundant; often to excess
      adv. profusely
      noun profuseness
      noun profusion
        Profuse vegetation makes jungle passage difficult.

155. **copious** adj. (kō′pē-əs)
    abundant
      adv. copiously
      noun copiousness
        The cupboard contains a copious supply of peanuts for snacking.

156. **stultify** verb (stul′tə-fī)
    1. to cause to appear absurd or foolish
    2. to make worthless
      noun stultification
      noun stultifier
        The prosecutor attempted to stultify the defendant's argument.

157. **zany** adj. (zā′nē)
    crazy; ridiculous; ludicrous; clownish
      adj. zanier—crazier
      adj. zaniest—craziest
        Her zebra skin jacket with the mink collar is absolutely zany.

158. **fatuous** adj. (fach′o͞o-əs)
    foolish; silly; inane; stupid
      adj. fatuitous
      adv. fatuously
      noun fatuousness
      noun fatuity (fə-to͞o′ə-tē)—utter foolishness;
                           a stupid remark
        Because his clothesline from the house to a
        pole sagged, fatuous Mr. Saphead spent
        $4,000 to have his house moved back.

159. **inane** adj. (in-ān′)
    foolish; silly; fatuous; empty-headed
      adv. inanely
        Ask an inane question, and you'll get an
        inane answer.

160. **sumph** noun (sumpf)
    a simpleton; a sullen person
        The big clumsy sumph rode a big clumsy
        horse.

161. **vacuous** adj. (vak′yo͞o-əs)
    1. stupid
    2. empty
      adv. vacuously
      noun vacuousness
      noun vacuity (va-kyo͞o′ə-tē)
        The vacuous boy locked his father in the
        refrigerator to get a cold pop.

162. **dolt** noun (dōlt)
    a stupid person
      adj. doltish
      adv. doltishly
      noun doltishness
        Have you heard about the dolt who stayed up all night to study for his blood test?

163. **insidious** adj. (in-sid′ē-əs)
    sly; crafty; cunning; treacherous
      adv. insidiously
      noun insidiousness
        Cancer is one of the most insidious diseases of mankind because it spreads without obvious symptoms.

164. **vulpine** adj. (vul′pin)
    sly; crafty; cunning; like a fox
        The vulpine businessman was justifiably reported to the "Better Business Bureau."

165. **wily** adj. (wi′lē)
    sly; crafty; cunning
      adj. wilier—slier
      adj. wiliest—sliest
      adv. wilily
      noun wiliness
        The fox is known and respected for his wily nature.

166. **cunning** adj. (kun′ing)
    crafty; shrewd; guileful
    adv. cunningly
    noun cunning—craftiness
    noun cunningness
    The cunning fox slipped through the chicken yard with nary (never) a disturbance.


167. **guileful** adj. (gīl′fəl)
    deceitful; full of trickery
    adv. guilefully
    noun guilefulness
    noun guile
    The guileful real estate salesman had his license revoked.

168. **chicanery** noun (shi-kā′nər-ē)
    trickery
    Advertising should be free of chicanery.

169. **subterfuge** noun (sub′tər-fyōōj)
    trickery; deception used to conceal a motive, escape a duty or avoid an issue
    An old method of subterfuge was used to separate the unsuspecting man from his money.

170. **artifice** noun (är′tə-fis)
    trickery
    The get-rich-quick idea was nothing more than an artifice employed to benefit the perpetrator.

171. **ruse** noun (ro͞oz)
    trickery
> Effective use of speed and ruse helped the smaller, less powerful football team win the league championship.

172. **wile** noun (wīl)
    trickery
    verb wile—to lure; to trick
> Hunters use wile by attracting ducks with decoys.

173. **duplicity** noun (do͞o-plis′ə-tē)
    trickery
> Unscrupulous contractors have used inferior materials and duplicity to sell their buildings.

174. **beguile** verb (bi-gīl′)
    1. to trick; to deceive
    2. to while away (time) pleasantly
    3. to charm or divert
    noun beguilement
    noun beguiler
> New paint on a car won't beguile an expert mechanic.

175. **mulct** verb (mulkt)
    to trick; to cheat
> The beguiler (deceiver) tried to mulct him of several hundred dollars.

176. **bilk** verb (bilk)
    to cheat; to deceive
        noun bilk—a trick; a fraud
        noun bilker
            Farmers he would often bilk, by selling
            them cows that wouldn't milk.

177. **hoodwink** verb (hŏod'wingk')
    to trick; to cheat; to deceive
        noun hoodwinker
            They who intentionally hoodwink, or have
            a criminal link, end up in the local clink.

178. **inveigle** verb (in-vē'gəl)
    to lure by trickery
        noun inveiglement
        noun inveigler
            Police tried to inveigle the crooks into a
            trap.

179. **belie** verb (bi-lī')
    to misrepresent; to disguise
        noun belier
            His shabby suits belie his millionaire
            status.

180. **dissemble** verb (di-sem'bəl)
    to conceal; to disguise
        adv. dissemblingly
        noun dissemblance
        noun dissembler
            A smile is a curve that can dissemble de-
            spair.

181. **ploy** noun (ploi)
    a maneuver
        The salesman used a guileful (deceitful) ploy to lure prospective customers.

182. **guileless** adj. (gĭl′lĭs)
    sincere; honest
        adv. guilelessly
        noun guilelessness
        Guileless persons are the opposite of guileful persons.

183. **illusion** noun (i-lo͞o′zhən)
    1. a false conception or vision formed by the imagination
    2. the act of deceiving
    3. something that deceives
    adj. illusional—deceptive, misleading
    adj. illusory
    adj. illusive
    adj. illusionary
    adv. illusively
    adv. illusorily
    noun illusiveness
    noun illusionism
    noun illusoriness
    noun illusionist
        He had the illusion that the dog was a growling grizzly bear.

184. **delusion** noun (di-lōō′zhən)
 1. a false belief or conviction
 2. the act of deceiving
 3. something that deceives
    adj. delusional
    adj. delusory
    adj. delusive
    adv. delusively
    noun delusiveness
    verb delude—to deceive
      He has the delusion that all politicians are corrupt.


185. **elusion** noun (i-lōō′zhən)
    act of escaping; act of eluding or evading
    adj. elusory
    adj. elusive
    adv. elusively
    noun elusiveness
    verb elude
      The convict was renowned (famous) as a master of elusion.


186. **allusion** noun (ə-lōō′zhən)
    a reference
    adj. allusive
    adv. allusively
    noun allusiveness
    verb allude
      Allusion to the horse facilitates (makes easier) description of the zebra.

187. **impassable** adj. (im-pas′ə-bəl)
    not passable
        adv. impassably
        noun impassibility
        noun impassableness
        noun impasse
            Muddy conditions make some country roads impassable.

188. **impassible** adj. (im-pas′ə-bəl)
    incapable of emotion
        adv. impassibly
        noun impassibility
        noun impassibleness
            The impassible hangman traveled from town to town.

189. **impassion** verb (im-pash′ən)
    to fill with emotion
            You impassion me with your sweet utterances.

190. **impassioned** adj. (im-pash′ənd)
    emotional; passionate
        adv. impassionedly
        noun impassionedness
            The lawyer made one last impassioned request that his client be found not guilty.

191. **germane** adj. (jər-mān′)
    pertinent; relevant; closely related
            Please make your comments germane to the question.

192. **pithy** adj. (pith'ē)
    expressed in few words; terse; full of meaning
      adj. pithier
      adj. pithiest
      adv. pithily
      noun pithiness
        Pithy reports are appreciated.


193. **laconic** adj. (lə-kon'ik)
    expressed in few words; extremely brief
      adj. laconical
      adv. laconically
      noun laconism
        Definitions in this book are purposely laconic.


194. **succint** adj. (sək-singkt')
    expressed in few words; concise; laconic
      adv. succintly
      noun succintness
        A loquacious (talkative) person finds difficulty in being succint.


195. **terse** adj. (tûrs)
    expressed in few words
      adj. terser
      adj. tersest
      adv. tersely
      noun terseness
        The minister preached a terse but excellent sermon.

196. **compendious** adj. (kəm-pen′dē-əs)
expressed in few words; concise
adv. compendiously
noun compendiousness
The paper gave a compendious account of
the new Broadway play.

197. **compendium** noun (kəm-pen′dē-əm)
a brief comprehensive summary
The teacher told the class to write a compendium of the novel.

198. **syllabus** noun (sil′ə-bəs)
concise statement of main points of a course of
study; brief summary at the beginning of a report
Be sure to read the syllabus before reading
the report.

199. **prolix** adj. (prō′liks)
long and wordy
adj. prolixity
adv. prolixly
noun prolixity
noun prolixness
A prolix speech is boring.

200. **verbose** adj. (vər-bōs′)
wordy
adv. verbosely
noun verboseness
noun verbosity—wordiness
The term paper was criticized for being
verbose.

# Test 2

1. aberrant  a. alert  b. cruel  c. intricate
   d. abnormal
2. accede  a. daze  b. gather  c. agree  d. entice
3. adventitious  a. awkward  b. elegant
   c. accidental  d. secretive
4. allusion  a. reference  b. image  c. magic
   d. false conception
5. anomalous  a. irregular  b. heavy  c. musical
   d. ornate
6. apparition  a. origin  b. shimmering light
   c. ghost  d. warning
7. artifice  a. dispute  b. ancient goods  c. trickery
   d. gossip
8. beguile  a. argue  b. postpone  c. trick
   d. take away
9. belie  a. isolate  b. swear  c. misrepresent
   d. accuse
10. bilk  a. seize  b. cheat  c. convince  d. deny
11. bombastic  a. explosive  b. exciting  c. showy
    d. huge
12. chicanery  a. connection  b. stimulus  c. chaos
    d. trickery
13. clandestine  a. curving  b. favorable  c. weary
    d. secret
14. commensurate  a. proportionate  b. beginning
    c. threatening  d. essential
15. compendious  a. roomy  b. concise
    c. humorous  d. perfect
16. compendium  a. summary  b. conversation
    c. treaty  d. spaciousness

17. concerted  a. combined  b. loud  c. stimulating
    d. deviant
18. conflagration  a. false idea  b. resentment
    c. celebration  d. fire
19. conjoin  a. unite  b. complain  c. dictate
    d. criticize
20. copious  a. crucial  b. abundant  c. effective
    d. greedy
21. covert  a. new  b. tearful  c. secret
    d. ill-smelling
22. cunning  a. quick  b. prompt  c. injurious
    d. crafty
23. delusion  a. vision  b. statement
    c. intelligence  d. false conception
24. derelict  a. neglectful  b. truthful
    c. easily understood  d. persistent
25. discophile  a. stamp collector  b. book lover
    c. phonograph collector  d. disco dancer
26. dissemble  a. compete  b. restore  c. retract
    d. conceal
27. dolt  a. dullard  b. custom  c. burden
    d. sadness
28. duplicity  a. double standard
    b. multiple dwelling  c. fear  d. trickery
29. elusion  a. garbage  b. reference
    c. act of lying  d. act of escaping
30. eminent  a. about to happen  b. squeamish
    c. tactful  d. distinguished
31. errant  a. stupid  b. silly  c. unpleasant
    d. wandering
32. facade  a. dishonesty  b. wild commotion
    c. building front  d. ideal place

33. fatuous  a. overweight  b. foolish
c. inappropriate  d. unpleasant
34. forgo  a. give up  b. travel  c. separate
d. ignore
35. fortuitous  a. famous  b. protected
c. accidental  d. worn out
36. furtive  a. animalistic  b. small  c. secret
d. fickle
37. germane  a. relevant  b. foreign  c. lengthy
d. stubborn
38. grandiloquent  a. vast  b. showy  c. pleasant
d. forceful
39. grandiose  a. widespread  b. magnificent
c. continuous  d. energetic
40. guileful  a. confusing  b. inactive  c. relaxed
d. deceitful
41. guileless  a. cranky  b. blunt  c. honest
d. insincere
42. histrionics  a. accusations  b. dramatics
c. accounts  d. recordations
43. holocaust  a. destruction  b. upheaval
c. festival  d. violence
44. hoodwink  a. postpone  b. blink  c. deprive
d. trick
45. illusion  a. something that deceives
b. act of escaping  c. sickness
d. something that is unbelievable
46. imminent  a. dangerous  b. close
c. comprehensible  d. wealthy
47. immoderate  a. unhealthy  b. excessive
c. disorderly  d. unequal
48. impassable  a. not passable  b. unemotional
c. very treacherous  d. unending

49. impassible   a. vivid   b. incapable of emotion
    c. highly improbable   d. not passable
50. impassion   a. make inferior
    b. fill with emotion   c. encourage goodwill
    d. wear away
51. impassioned   a. perceptive   b. uncontrollable
    c. weariness   d. passionate
52. inadvertent   a. moving   b. frantic   c. negligent
    d. ashamed
53. inane   a. precise   b. foolish   c. retarded
    d. flawless
54. inchoate   a. hidden   b. beginning   c. malicious
    d. original
55. incipient   a. dull   b. abnormal   c. early stage
    d. late
56. inordinate   a. crude   b. overwhelming
    c. excessive   d. impressive
57. inperpetuum   a. forever   b. royal   c. between
    d. meaningless
58. insidious   a. crazy   b. crafty   c. colorful
    d. ridiculous
59. intemperate   a. excessive   b. mild   c. harsh
    d. wild
60. inveigle   a. defeat   b. generate   c. speculate
    d. lure
61. itinerant   a. metallic   b. shiny   c. hectic
    d. wandering
62. laconic   a. definitive   b. authentic   c. wordy
    d. pithy
63. latent   a. open   b. meaningless   c. bitter
    d. concealed
64. moor   a. induce   b. exchange   c. loosen
    d. secure

65. mulct  a. make up  b. absorb  c. create  d. trick
66. numismatist  a. art collector  b. driller
    c. coin collector  d. newcomer
67. ostensible  a. unknown  b. mistaken
    c. harmonious  d. genuine
68. ostensive  a. apparent  b. inconspicuous
    c. brilliant  d. lavish
69. ostentatious  a. showy  b. upright
    c. transparent  d. flawless
70. palpable  a. tasty  b. obvious  c. feeble
    d. smooth
71. patent  a. apparent  b. warning  c. reasonable
    d. savory
72. philatelist  a. slow person
    b. one who meditates  c. stamp collector
    d. one who deserts faith
73. pithy  a. woody  b. terse  c. talkative
    d. studious
74. plethoric  a. twisting  b. scarce  c. overfull
    d. innocent
75. ploy  a. understatement  b. maneuver
    c. agressiveness  d. nearness
76. pompous  a. subduable  b. coarse  c. showy
    d. silent
77. pontificate  a. to act enthusiastically  b. write
    c. to act quickly
    d. to speak in a stylish manner
78. pretentious  a. showy  b. quiet  c. new  d. brisk
79. pretermit  a. caution  b. perplex  c. overlook
    d. beg
80. profuse  a. reserved  b. abundant  c. heavy
    d. winding

81. prolix  a. short and sweet  b. expert
    c. long and wordy  d. empty
82. ratable  a. fair  b. avoidable  c. unequal
    d. proportional
83. rhetorical  a. stylish  b. foolish  c. political
    d. spontaneous
84. ruse  a. debris  b. trickery  c. fault  d. magician
85. salient  a. sedate  b. peaceful  c. conspicuous
    d. reclining
86. stultify  a. to make loud  b. to make bitter
    c. to make illegal  d. to make absurd
87. subterfuge  a. trickery  b. sabotage
    c. destruction  d. fire
88. succint  a. limited  b. concise  c. vague
    d. restrictive
89. sumph  a. water pump  b. fake art
    c. simpleton  d. rumor
90. sumptuous  a. superficial  b. fragile  c. ugly
    d. superb
91. surreptitious  a. favorable  b. skillful  c. sleepy
    d. secret
92. syllabus  a. pronunciation  b. puzzle
    c. summary  d. nonsense
93. terse  a. vigorous  b. pithy  c. affectionate
    d. level
94. vacillating  a. wavering  b. responsible
    c. steady  d. indifferent
95. vacuous  a. stupid  b. small  c. sly  d. sparkling
96. verbose  a. loquacious  b. wordy
    c. conclusive  d. whimsical
97. vulpine  a. slender  b. cowlike  c. foxy
    d. odd

98. wile  a. trace  b. explosion  c. attraction
    d. trickery
99. wily  a. eccentric  b. quaint  c. fancy
    d. cunning
100. zany  a. extraordinary  b. lavish  c. ridiculous
    d. unnecessary

| | | | |
|---|---|---|---|
| 1. d | 26. d | 51. d | 76. c |
| 2. c | 27. a | 52. c | 77. d |
| 3. c | 28. d | 53. b | 78. a |
| 4. a | 29. d | 54. b | 79. c |
| 5. a | 30. d | 55. c | 80. b |
| 6. c | 31. d | 56. c | 81. c |
| 7. c | 32. c | 57. a | 82. d |
| 8. c | 33. b | 58. b | 83. a |
| 9. c | 34. a | 59. a | 84. b |
| 10. b | 35. c | 60. d | 85. c |
| 11. c | 36. c | 61. d | 86. d |
| 12. d | 37. a | 62. d | 87. a |
| 13. d | 38. b | 63. d | 88. b |
| 14. a | 39. b | 64. d | 89. c |
| 15. b | 40. d | 65. d | 90. d |
| 16. a | 41. c | 66. c | 91. d |
| 17. a | 42. b | 67. d | 92. c |
| 18. d | 43. a | 68. a | 93. b |
| 19. a | 44. d | 69. a | 94. a |
| 20. b | 45. a | 70. b | 95. a |
| 21. c | 46. b | 71. a | 96. b |
| 22. d | 47. b | 72. c | 97. c |
| 23. d | 48. a | 73. b | 98. d |
| 24. a | 49. b | 74. c | 99. d |
| 25. c | 50. b | 75. b | 100. c |

## SCORING

Correct answers

    100-90=A (excellent)
     89-80=B (good)
     79-70=C (fair)
     69-60=D (poor)
     59- 0=E (Start over!)

Score before word study _____
Score after word study _____

201. **superfluous** adj. (soo-pûr'floo-əs)
   excessively abundant; unnecessary; irrelevant
   adv. superfluously
   noun superfluousness
   noun superfluity
      No superfluous questions please!


202. **redundant** adj. (ri-dun'dənt)
   superabundant; excessive; wordy
   adv. redundantly
   noun redundance
   noun redundancy
      "I hate to be redundant," said the teacher,
      "but, for the tenth time, don't forget the
      quiz Friday."


203. **tedious** adj. (tē'dē-əs)
   long and tiresome; boring
   adv. tediously
   noun tediousness
   noun tedium
      Those who are impatient find fishing tedi-
      ous while those who are patient find it re-
      laxing.


204. **proclivity** noun (prō-kliv'ə-tē)
   a natural tendency; a propensity; an inclination
      The hypochondriac has a proclivity to
      complain about his health.

205. **propensity** noun (prə-pen′sə-tē)
   1. a natural tendency; a proclivity
   2. a partiality
         He who has a propensity for accidents will
         have high insurance premiums.


206. **predilection** noun (prē′-də-lek′shən)
   1. a preference for something
   2. a partiality
         Do you have a predilection for a particular
         cuisine (style of cooking)?


207. **penchant** noun (pen′chənt)
      a strong inclination; a taste for something
         Obese (fat) Orville has a penchant for
         chocolate marshmallow ice cream.


208. **predisposition** noun (pre′dis-pə-zish′ən)
      a tendency
         High cholesterol has a predisposition to
         cause premature death.


209. **predispose** verb (prē′dis-pōz′)
      to make susceptible
         High cholesterol will predispose one to
         premature death.

210. **tendentious** adj. (ten-den'shəs)
    having or showing a definite tendency, aim or
    bias; biased
        adv. tendentiously
        noun tendentiousness
            The comedy act was a tendentious political
            promotion.

211. **propinquity** noun (prō ping'kwə-tē)
    nearness
            People sense his propinquity because of
            a strong, offensive body odor.

212. **impavid** adj. (im-pav'id)
    fearless; intrepid; bold
        adv. impavidly
        noun impavidity
            The badger is known as an impavid fighter.

213. **intrepid** adj. (in-trep'id)
    fearless; dauntless
        adv. intrepidly
        noun intrepidity
            The intrepid regiment rode toward the
            enemy with haste.

214. **dauntless** adj. (dônt'lis)
    fearless
        adv. dauntlessly
        noun dauntlessness
            Some called the daredevil driver dauntless,
            while others called him stupid.

215. **temerarious** adj. (tem′ə-râr′ē-əs)
   reckless; bold; rash
     adv. temerariously
     noun temerariousness
     noun temerity
       Drunkenness begets (produces) temerari-
       ous conduct.

216. **reprieve** noun (ri-prēv′)
   a temporary delay from execution; a postponement; a temporary relief
     adj. reprievable
     verb reprieve—to grant a delay from execu-
                 tion; to postpone; to delay
       The governor has the power to grant a
       criminal a reprieve from execution.

217. **respite** noun (res′pit)
   a temporary relief; a postponement; a period of rest
   rest
     verb respite—to postpone
       The ten-minute break is a cherished respite
       from assembly line doldrums (dullness).

218. **repose** verb (ri-pōz′)
   to rest; to lay down
     adv. reposeful
     noun reposefulness
     noun reposal
     noun reposer
     noun repose—a state of rest; calmness
       Those who repose all day,
       have no way of earning pay.

219. **diatribe** noun (dī′ə-trib)
   a bitter discussion; an abusive discourse
   > Two senators got involved in a heated diat-
   > ribe.

220. **querulous** adj. (kwer′ə ləs)
   full of complaints; fretful; petulant; faultfinding
   adv. querulously
   noun querulousness
   > The querulous party-goer complained he
   > had seen more excitement at the opening of
   > a window.

221. **captious** adj. (kap′shəs)
   faultfinding; having a criticizing nature
   adv. captiously
   noun captiousness
   > The captious boarder complained his attic
   > room was so low the mice were hunch-
   > backed.

222. **niggling** adj. (nig′ling)
   1. annoying; nagging
   2. fussy; over precise
   adv. nigglingly
   verb niggle
   > She is the most niggling person in the club.

223. **irascible** adj. (i-ras′ə-bəl)
    easily angered; quick-tempered
      adv. irascibly
      noun irascibility
      noun irascibleness
        The irascible landlord threatened to evict
        the tenants when their dog barked.

224. **testy** adj. (tes′tē)
    easily angered; quick-tempered
      adv. testily
      noun testiness
        The slightest noise causes the testy man
        upstairs to stomp his feet.

225. **choleric** adj. (kol′ər-ik)
    easily angered; quick-tempered
        Scorpio women have choleric dispositions,
        according to astrologists.

226. **peevish** adj. (pē′vish)
    irritable; querulous; cross; petulant
      adv. peevishly
      noun peevishness
      verb peeve—to make peevish
        The loquacious (talkative) students trans-
        formed her into a peevish teacher.

227. **petulant** adj. (pech′ o͞o-lənt)
    querulous; irritable; showing irritation over a
    small annoyance
      adj. petulantly
      noun petulance
      noun petulancy
        A petulant person is difficult to tolerate.

228. **fractious** adj. (frak'shəs)
unruly; irritable; easily angered
adv. fractiously
noun fractiousness
A fractious bull broke his chain and chased the judge from the show ring.


229. **bumptious** adj. (bum'shəs)
offensively self-asserting; offensively putting forth one's self, ideas or wishes
adv. bumptiously
noun bumptiousness
Because of his bumptious mannerisms, classmates call him a "show off ."


230. **refractory** adj. (ri-frak'tər-ē)
rebellious; unruly; obstinate; unmanageable; not amenable
adv. refractorily
noun refractoriness
He is such a refractory kid none of the reform schools even want him.


231. **contentious** adj. (kən-ten'shəs)
quarrelsome
adv. contentiously
noun contentiousness
Without a nap the two-year-old became contentious.

232. **perverse** adj. (pər-vûrs′)
obstinate; deviating from the normal; cranky
adv. perversely
noun perverseness
He is so perverse that he kills time by
smashing people's wrist watches.

233. **recalcitrant** adj. (ri-kal′sə-trənt)
rebellious; unruly; obstinate; unmanageable
noun recalcitrant—one who is rebellious
noun recalcitrance
noun recalcitrancy
verb recalcitrate—to refuse to co-operate
Recalcitrant students receive poor citizen-
ship grades.

234. **insurgent** adj. (in-sûr′jənt)
rebellious
noun insurgent—a rebel
noun insurgence
noun insurgency
The insurgent leader advocated the overthrow of the current dictator.

235. **seditious** adj. (si-dish′əs)
rebellious; tending to cause discontent among
people
adj. seditionary
adv. seditiously
noun seditiousness
noun sedition
noun seditionist
The seditious tactics of anti-government
organizations are carefully monitored.

236. **pugnacious** adj. (pug-nā′shəs)
   quarrelsome
      adv. pugnaciously
      noun pugnaciousness
      noun pugnacity
         The pugnacious neighbor has fought with
         everybody on the block.


237. **bellicose** adj. (bel′ə-kōs)
   warlike; pugnacious
      adv. bellicosely
      noun bellicosity
         The bellicose tribe was constantly at war.


238. **termagant** noun (tûr′mə-gənt)
   a violent and quarrelsome woman
      adj. termagant—quarrelsome
      noun termagancy
         The demure (reserved) young lady turned
         into a termagant after marriage.


239. **truculent** adj. (truk′yə-lənt)
   aggressive; savage; hostile
      adv. truculently
      noun truculence
      noun truculency
         Escape of the truculent lion created fear
         within the neighborhood.

240. **inimical** adj. (in-im′i-kəl)
    unfriendly; hostile; adverse
    adv. inimically
    noun inimicality
        Inimical powers continue to fight for control.


241. **willful** adj. (wil′fəl)
    1. intentional
    2. headstrong; obstinate
    adv. willfully
    noun willfulness
        The willful burro would not move from the road.


242. **intractable** adj. (in-trak′tə-bəl)
    stubborn; unruly
        adv. intractably
        noun intractability
        noun intractableness
            Rodeo managements search for broncos with intractable dispositions.


243. **obstreperous** adj. (əb-strəp′ər-əs)
    unruly; noisy
        adv. obstreperously
        noun obstreperousness
            The obstreperous student was suspended from school.

244. **contumacious** adj. (kon′tōō-mā′shəs)
   disobedient; rebellious
   adv. contumaciously
   noun contumaciousness
   The sedate (calm) audience turned into a contumacious mob when the rock star failed to appear.

245. **insubordinate** adj. (in′sə-bôr′də-nit)
   disobedient; rebellious
   adv. insubordinately
   noun insubordinate—a rebellious person
   noun insubordination
   The employee was fired for insubordinate behavior.

246. **restive** adj. (res′tiv)
   1. rebellious; unruly
   2. restless; uneasy
   adv. restively
   noun restiveness
   People accustomed to democracy would be restive under a communistic dictatorship.

247. **egregious** adj. (i-grē′jəs)
   conspicuously bad; prominent in a bad sense
   adv. egregiously
   noun egregiousness
   The newspaper reporter made an egregious mistake by not presenting the facts correctly.

248. **infamous** adj. (ĭn'fə-məs)
bad; of evil fame; having bad reputation
adv. infamously
noun infamousness
noun infamy
We've all heard of Al Capone and his infamous gang.


249. **notorious** adj. (nō-tôr'ē-əs)
well-known in an unfavorable sense
adv. notoriously
noun notoriety
The notorious coral snake is of utmost concern to hikers in southern states.


250. **incorrigible** adj. (ĭn-kôr'ə-jə bəl)
bad beyond correction; beyond reformation
adv. incorrigibly
noun incorrigibility
noun incorrigibleness
Incorrigible youths are destined to become inhabitants of our state penitentaries.


251. **odious** adj. (ō'dē-əs)
offensive; cruel; disgusting; exciting hate or disgust
adv. odiously
noun odiousness
noun odium
Swinging a cat by the tail is definitely an odious act.

252. **invidious** adj. (in-vid′ē-əs)
   creating dislike; offensive; provoking anger; repugnant
       adv. invidiously
       noun invidiousness
           The realtor used invidious tactics to get
           people to sell their homes.


253. **iniquitous** adj. (in-ik′wə-təs)
   wicked; unjust
       adv. iniquitously
       noun iniquitousness
       noun iniquity (in-ik′wə-te)
           Robin Hood is known for his relentless
           (continuous) fight against the iniquitous
           tax collectors.


254. **sinister** adj. (sin′is-tər)
   evil; wicked
       adv. sinisterly
       noun sinisterness
           Batman and Robin are devoted to foiling
           the sinister plots of criminals.


255. **heinous** adj. (hā′nəs)
   extremely wicked or evil
       adv. heinously
       noun heinousness
           The city recorded another heinous crime.

256. **atrocious** adj. (ə-trō′shəs)
extremely wicked or cruel
adv. atrociously
noun atrociousness
noun atrocity (ə-tros′ə-tē)
Atrocious killing techniques were practiced by meat-packing companies in years past.


257. **nefarious** adj. (ni-fâr′ē-əs)
extremely evil; extremely wicked
adv. nefariously
noun nefariousness
The book about witchcraft was filled with nefarious activities.


258. **diabolic** adj. (di′ə-bol′ik)
atrociously wicked
adj. diabolical
adv. diabolically
noun diabolicalness
It was diabolic of the child to pull the wings off the butterfly.


259. **horrendous** adj. (hô-ren′dəs)
horrible; frightful; dreadful
adv. horrendously
Stock market prices took a horrendous drop last week.

260. **vile** adj. (vīl)
> repulsive; bad; obnoxious; base; wicked
>> adv. vilely
>> noun vileness
>>> Vile treatment in a concentration camp destroyed the will of the once strong leader.

261. **repugnant** adj. (ri-pug′nənt)
> offensive; repulsive
>> noun repugnance
>> noun repugnancy
>>> The repugnant drunk was kicked off the bus.

262. **abhorrent** adj. (ab-hôr′ənt)
> repugnant; detestable; offensive
>> adv. abhorrently
>> noun abhorrence
>> noun abhorrer
>> verb abhor—to dislike strongly
>>> His abhorrent eating habits left him eating alone.

263. **abominable** adj. (ə-bom′in-ə-bəl)
> repugnant; detestable; offensive, bad
>> adv. abominably
>> noun abominableness
>> verb abominate—to dislike strongly
>>> Some people think taxes are abominable, forgetting what it would be like without them.

264. **loathsome** adj. (lōth′səm)
    repugnant; detestable; offensive
        adj. loathly
        adj. loathful
        adv. loathfully
        adv. loathingly
        adv. loathsomely
        noun loathing—an extreme disgust
        noun loather
        noun loathfulness
        noun loathsomeness
        verb loathe
            The country is disturbed by the loathsome activities of criminals.

265. **calamitous** adj. (kə-lam′ə-təs)
    unfavorable; disastrous
        adv. calamitously
        noun calamitousness
        noun calamity—a disaster
            The visiting team suffered a calamitous defeat.

266. **deplorable** adj. (di-plôr′ə-bəl)
    wretched; lamentable; sad; regrettable
        adv. deplorably
        noun deplorableness
        noun deplorability
        verb deplore—to express grief or regret
            It's deplorable the way the neighbor beats his dog.

267. **lamentable** adj. (lə-mənt′ə-bəl)
    deplorable; regrettable
        adj. lamented—mourned for (for one who is
                dead)
        adj. lamenting
        adv. lamentably
        adv. lamentingly
        noun lamentation
        noun lamentableness
        noun lamenter
        noun lament—an expression of sorrow or re-
                gret
        verb lament—to feel sorrow or regret
        His heavy business investment was a la-
        mentable failure.

268. **adverse** adj. (ad-vûrs′)
    1. unfavorable
    2. opposed
        adv. adversely
        noun adverseness
        noun adversity—a condition of hardship
        He is sensitive to adverse (unfavorable)
        criticism.

269. **turpitude** noun (tûr′pə-to͞od)
    corruption; depravity
        Moral turpitude has brought down the
        most powerful of men.

270. **ignoble** adj. (ig-nō′bəl)
dishonorable in purpose or character
adv. ignobly
noun ignobility
noun ignobleness
The ignoble team of Bonnie and Clyde killed impassively (not feeling emotion).

271. **base** adj. (bās)
morally low; mean; contemptible
adv. basely
noun baseness
He is so base and disgusting that when he stands on the ocean front, the tide won't even come in.

272. **ignominious** adj. (ig′nə-min′ē-əs)
shameful; humiliating; disgraceful; despicable
adv. ignominously
noun ignominiousness
noun ignominy—disgracefulness
The erstwhile (former) world champion boxer quickly retreated to the locker room after his ignominious loss to an unknown.

273. **despicable** adj. (des′pi-kə-bəl)
mean; vile; contemptible
adv. despicably
noun despicability
noun despicableness
The despicable old recluse (one who lives in seclusion) shoots at trespassers.

274. **contemptible** adj. (kən-temp′tə-bəl)
despicable; sarcastic; bitter
adv. contemptibly
noun contemptibility
noun contemptibleness
Contemptible behavior is not tolerated in private schools.

275. **acrimonious** adj. (ak′rə-mō′nē-əs)
sarcastic; very bitter
adv. acrimoniously
noun acrimoniousness
noun acrimony
When the acrimonious clerk was fired, business began to flourish.

276. **asperity** noun (as-per′ə-te)
1. bitterness or sharpness of temper
2. hardship; difficulty
The performer's retort, shouted with asperity, shocked the hecklers into a quiet state of disbelief.

277. **acerbity** noun (ə sûr′bə-tē)
bitterness; a sharp temper
noun acerbitude
The remarks, spoken with acerbity, caused those to whom they were directed much public embarrassment.

278. **vitriolic** adj. (vit'rē-ol'ik)
 1. severely sarcastic; sharp; caustic
 2. burning
    noun vitriol
       Vitriolic criticism often involves
       heightened emotions.

279. **caustic** adj. (kôs'tik)
    bitter; sarcastic
       adv. caustically
       noun causticity
          Caustic remarks were voiced over the in-
          creased tax rates.

280. **mordant** adj. (mor'dənt)
    bitter; sarcastic
       noun mordancy
          He has a mordant wit as evidenced by his
          sick ethnic jokes.

281. **mordacious** adj. (môr-dā'shəs)
    sarcastic; biting
       adv. mordaciously
       noun mordacity
          The editor's mordacious pen alienated
          many readers.

282. **sardonic** adj. (sär-don'ik)
    bitter; sarcastic; sneering
       adv. sardonically
       noun sardonicism
          A sardonic man married a mordant (bitter)
          woman and they had four little caustic
          (sarcastic) brats.

283. **cynical** adj. (sin′i-kəl)
    bitter; sarcastic; sneering; faultfinding
      adv. cynically
      noun cynicism
      noun cynicalness
      noun cynic—a faultfinding person
        Don't be cynical of the program, instead
        make suggestions for its improvement.

284. **contemptuous** adj. (kən-temp′cho͞o-əs)
    bitter; sarcastic; scornful
      adv. contemptuously
      noun contemptuousness
        Let rejection make you inquisitive (curi-
        ous), not contemptuous.

285. **vituperative** adj. (vī-to͞o′pər-ə-tiv)
    abusive; berating; scolding
      adj. vituperatively
      noun vituperation—abusive language or the
                      act of berating
      noun vituperator
      verb vituperate—to berate
        Vituperative language in gangster movies
        is commonplace.

286. **derogatory** adj. (di-rog′-ə-tôr′ē)
     belittling
         adj. derogative
         adv. derogatively
         adv. derogatorily
         noun derogatoriness
         verb derogate (der′ə gāt)—to belittle
         It's hard to imagine sweet old grandma uttering a derogatory remark.

287. **disparaging** adj. (dis-par′ij-ing)
     belittling
         adv. disparagingly
         noun disparagement
         noun disparager
         verb disparage—to belittle
         The farm leader's disparaging speech criticized the trend toward subdividing agricultural land.

288. **vindictive** adj. (vin-dik′tiv)
     revengeful; tending to hold grudges
         adv. vindictively
         noun vindictiveness
         The convicted prisoner shouted vindictive threats at the jury.

289. **malevolent** adj. (mə-lev′ə-lənt)
     wishing evil on others; malicious
         adv. malevolently
         noun malevolence
         "Malevolent talk such as that belongs in horror movies, not here in the classroom," stated the teacher.

290. **malicious** adj. (mə-lish′əs)
   wishing or doing damage or evil to another's
   person or property
      adv. maliciously
      noun maliciousness
      noun malice—the desire to injure or damage
         That kid was responsible for the malicious
         destruction of the street sign.


291. **boorish** adj. (bŏor′ish)
   rude; ill-mannered
      adv. boorishly
      noun boorishness
      noun boor
         Boorish students get expelled.


292. **crass** adj. (kras)
   vulgar; stupid; rude; unrefined
      adv. crassly
      noun crassness
      noun crassitude—stupidity; rudeness
         He wore his work boots to the dance—how
         crass.


293. **churlish** adj. (chûr′lish)
   rude; ill-mannered
      adv. churlishly
      noun churlishness
         He was told, "Either repress [restrain]
         your churlish manners or leave the
         premises."

294. **surly** adj. (sûr′lē)
rude; gruff
adv. surlily
noun surliness
He was dirty and burly (large bodysize)
with mannerisms surely surly.

295. **loutish** adj. (lou′tish)
rude; ill-mannered; clumsy; stupid
adv. loutishly
noun loutishness
noun lout
The loutish drunk asked passers-by for
their spare change.

296. **uncouth** adj. (un-kōōth′)
unmannerly; crude; unrefined; lacking grace
adv. uncouthly
noun uncouthness
Because of his uncouth table manners, no-
body wanted to eat with him.

297. **ungainly** adj. (un-gān′lē)
awkward; unrefined; lacking grace
noun ungainliness
The ungainly little girl grew into a graceful
young lady.

298. **proverbial** adj. (prə-vûr′bē-əl)
well-known; being an object of common mention
adv. proverbially
Stories of Paul Bunyan and his proverbial
blue-ox, Babe, have delighted many
youngsters.

299. **renowned** adj. (ri-nound´)
   famous
   noun renown—fame
   She collects autographs from renowned
   rock and roll singers.

300. **invective** noun (in-vek´tiv)
   a vituperation; a violent accusation; a wordy
   abuse
   adj. invective—abusive
   adv. invectively
   noun invectiveness
   The old recluse gave the trespassing real
   estate salesman an unforgettable invective.

1. abhorrent  a. wavering  b. offensive  c. casual
   d. bewildering
2. abominable  a. detestable  b. native  c. gastric
   d. mountainous
3. acerbity  a. enthusiasm  b. bitterness
   c. closeness  d. calmness
4. acrimonious  a. confusing  b. sarcastic
   c. enlightening  d. envious
5. adverse  a. musical  b. unfavorable
   c. desirous  d. unlike
6. asperity  a. bitterness  b. wealth  c. poverty
   d. ignorance
7. atrocious  a. wicked  b. illuminating  c. sharp
   d. belligerent
8. base  a. steadfast  b. supporting
   c. inexperienced  d. contemptible
9. bellicose  a. tinkling  b. warlike  c. biased
   d. talented
10. boorish  a. stunned  b. piggish  c. rude
    d. modest
11. bumptious  a. self-destructive  b. self-asserting
    c. rough  d. sleazy
12. calamitous  a. balmy  b. peaceful
    c. frightening  d. disastrous
13. captious  a. helpful  b. diligent  c. flexible
    d. faultfinding
14. caustic  a. satisfied  b. positive  c. sticky
    d. sarcastic
15. choleric  a. quick-tempered  b. fat
    c. continuous  d. slow starter

16. churlish  a. quarrelsome  b. boorish
    c. lightheaded  d. flimsy
17. contemptible    a. despicable  b. gloomy
    c. foul  d fussy
18. contemptuous  a. windy  b. fickle  c. bitter
    d. sweet
19. contentious  a. quarrelsome  b. mystical
    c. wholesome  d. aware
20. contumacious  a. easygoing  b. full of vigor
    c. disobedient  d. comical
21. crass  a. swollen  b. luxurious  c. rude
    d. charming
22. cynical  a. delightful  b. shapeless  c. sneering
    d. tiresome
23. dauntless  a. accomplished  b. competent
    c. becoming  d. fearless
24. deplorable  a. daring  b. regrettable
    c. hilarious  d. stirring
25. derogatory  a. belittling  b. powerful  c. insane
    d. common
26. despicable  a. mean  b. smart  c. capable
    d. efficient
27. diabolic  a. wicked  b. dynamic  c. harmless
    d. worldly
28. diatribe  a. settlement  b. bitter discussion
    c. sailing vessel  d. desertion of principles
29. disparaging  a. unusual  b. willing
    c. astonishing  d. belittling
30. egregious  a. pleasantly surprised
    b. conspicuously bad  c. crowd  loving
    d. popular

31. fractious  a. unruly  b. broken  c. displeased
    d. horrified
32. heinous  a. upsetting  b. wicked  c. worried
    d. glad
33. horrendous  a. horrible  b. apologetic
    c. burdensome  d. touching
34. ignoble  a. overjoyed  b. dishonorable
    c. satisfying  d. gorgeous
35. ignominious  a. terrific  b. elegant  c. shameful
    d. nameless
36. impavid  a. awful  b. angry  c. sleepy
    d. fearless
37. incorrigible  a. indebted  b. very large
    c. extremely bad  d. primitive
38. infamous  a. colossal  b. bad  c. ancient
    d. unknown
39. inimical  a. hostile  b. aged  c. permissible
    d. friendly
40. iniquitous  a. impartial  b. unjust
    c. everlasting  d. rowdy
41. insubordinate  a. continual  b. below
    c. disobedient  d. laughable
42. insurgent  a. unending  b. sneaky  c. candid
    d. rebellious
43. intractable  a. stubborn  b. rash  c. deep
    d. idiotic
44. intrepid  a. jealous  b. pensive  c. dull
    d. dauntless
45. invective  a. speed  b. thoughtlessness
    c. vision  d. accusation
46. invidious  a. offensive  b. likeable  c. lewd
    d. scholastic

47. irascible  a. difficult to perform  b. disastrous
    c. thick  d. quick-tempered
48. lamentable  a. useful  b. visible  c. deplorable
    d. important
49. loathsome  a. repugnant  b. lazy  c. strong
    d. sane
50. loutish  a. plump  b. clumsy
    c. disgusting to smell  d. sporadic
51. malevolent  a. malicious  b. slighted  c. manly
    d. simple
52. malicious  a. unsuitable
    b. wishing or doing evil
    c. unconcerned  d. causing chaos
53. mordacious  a. masterful  b. sarcastic
    c. deadly  d. dishonest
54. mordant  a. apparent  b. bitter  c. poisonous
    d. regretful
55. nefarious  a. stingy  b. indispensable  c. evil
    d. meat-eating
56. niggling  a. different  b. cultural  c. annoying
    d. distinctive
57. notorious  a. frank  b. leading  c. well-known
    d. blissful
58. obstreperous  a. allowable  b. unruly  c. open
    d. mediocre
59. odious  a. dainty  b. smelly  c. strict
    d. disgusting
60. peevish  a. irritable  b. rational  c. quaint
    d. little
61. penchant  a. faith  b. inclination  c. writing
    d. aid
62. perverse  a. obvious  b. limited  c. obstinate
    d. stationary

63. petulant  a. fixed  b. mutual  c. enthralled
    d. irritable
64. predilection  a. process  b. procrastinator
    c. partiality  d. lack
65. predispose  a. to digest  b. to make susceptible
    c. to cause to rot  d. to expire early
66. predisposition  a. behavior  b. tendency
    c. discription  d. payment
67. proclivity  a. despair  b. inclination
    c. early civilization  d. excellence
68. propensity  a. partiality  b. earnestness
    c. relief  d. profit
69. propinquity  a. nearness  b. old-time
    c. tendency  d. carefulness
70. proverbial  a. well-known  b. wordy
    c. rambling  c. uninteresting
71. pugnacious  a. occasional  b. polished
    c. quarrelsome  d. lively
72. querulous  a. faultfinding  b. unusual
    c. obscure  d. fierce
73. recalcitrant  a. invalid  b. unclassifiable
    c. ugly  d. unmanageable
74. redundant  a. discarded  b. boastful
    c. excessive  d. substantial
75. refractory  a. artistic  b. rebellious  c. bent
    d. rustic
76. renowned  a. famous  b. useless  c. indebted
    d. poverty-stricken
77. repose  a. rest  b. stand  c. frustrate
    d. demonstrate
78. reprieve  a. desertion  b. relief  c. murder
    d. prison

79. repugnant  a. repetitive  b. inspiring
    c. repulsive  d. unalterable
80. respite  a. stupidity  b. obediency  d. quietness
    d. relief
81. restive  a. untrustworthy  b. silent  c. unruly
    d. cruel
82. sardonic  a. sarcastic  b. enraged
    c. peace-loving  d. sole
83. seditious  a. rebellious  b. respected
    c. inaccurate  d. sitting
84. sinister  a. bloody  b. evil  c. uneven
    d. faultfinding
85. superfluous  a. superhuman  b. unnecessary
    c. smooth  d. futile
86. surly  a. untimely  b. well-known  c. stern
    d. rude
87. tedious  a. healthful  b. unbearable  c. morose
    d. boring
88. temerarious  a. disliked  b. shy  c. inadequate
    d. reckless
89. tendentious  a. slow moving
    b. sleep-producing  c. very important
    d. having aim
90. termagant  a. secluded  b. thrifty
    c. quarrelsome  d. ignorant
91. testy  a. noisy  b. unyielding
    c. quick-tempered  d.proven
92. truculent  a. hostile  b. elaborate  c. costly
    d. lustful
93. turpitude  a. verdict  b. corruption
    c. contentment  d. knowledge
94. uncouth  a. memorized  b. crude  c. exposed
    d. flabby

95. ungainly  a. playful  b. detestable  c. lost
    d. awkward
96. vile  a. obnoxious  b. sweet  c. narrow
    d. suffering
97. vindictive  a. conquerable  b. intense
    c. crazed  d. revengeful
98. vitriolic  a. enlarged  b. misunderstood
    c. sarcastic  d. angry
99. vituperative  a. harmful  b. unfortunate
    c. abusive  d. impatient
100. willful  a. hasty  b. headstrong  c. easily
     managed  d. severe

# Test 3

## Answers

| | | | |
|---|---|---|---|
| 1. b | 26. a | 51. a | 76. a |
| 2. a | 27. a | 52. b | 77. a |
| 3. b | 28. b | 53. b | 78. b |
| 4. b | 29. d | 54. b | 79. c |
| 5. b | 30. b | 55. c | 80. d |
| 6. a | 31. a | 56. c | 81. c |
| 7. a | 32. b | 57. c | 82. a |
| 8. d | 33. a | 58. b | 83. a |
| 9. b | 34. b | 59. d | 84. b |
| 10. c | 35. c | 60. a | 85. b |
| 11. b | 36. d | 61. b | 86. d |
| 12. d | 37. c | 62. c | 87. d |
| 13. d | 38. b | 63. d | 88. d |
| 14. d | 39. a | 64. c | 89. d |
| 15. a | 40. b | 65. b | 90. c |
| 16. b | 41. c | 66. b | 91. c |
| 17. a | 42. d | 67. b | 92. a |
| 18. c | 43. a | 68. a | 93. b |
| 19. a | 44. d | 69. a | 94. b |
| 20. c | 45. d | 70. a | 95. d |
| 21. c | 46. a | 71. c | 96. a |
| 22. c | 47. d | 72. a | 97. d |
| 23. d | 48. c | 73. d | 98. c |
| 24. b | 49. a | 74. c | 99. c |
| 25. a | 50. b | 75. b | 100. b |

## SCORING

Correct answers
- 100-90 = A (excellent)
- 89-80 = B (good)
- 79-70 = C (fair)
- 69-60 = D (poor)
- 59- 0 = E (Start over!)

Score before word study _____

Score after word study _____

301. **inveigh** verb (in-vā′)
    to attack with words (use with against)
        noun inveigher
           Communists inveigh against democracy.


302. **lustful** adj (lust′fəl)
    1. driven by sexual desire
    2. driven by desire to possess or enjoy
        adv. lustfully
        noun lustfulness
        noun lust—followed by "for" or "of" as in
              the lust for power
        verb lust—followed by "for" or "after."
              They lust after power.
        Many magazines cater to man's lustful appetite.


303. **libidinous** adj. (li-bid′ə-nəs)
    excessive sexual desire, lustful
        adv. libidinously
        noun libidinousness
           His openly libidinous behavior caused
           objections from the neighbors.


304. **lascivious** adj. (lə-siv′ē-əs)
    arousing sensual desire; lustful; lewd
        adv. lasciviously
        noun lasciviousness
           Having appeared in several centerfolds,
           the starlet soon became stereotyped as lascivious.

305. **dissolute** adj. (dis′ə-lo͞ot)
    morally loose
        adv. dissolutely
        noun dissoluteness
            Dissolute societies have a history of transitoriness (temporariness).


306. **licentious** adj. (lī-sen′shəs)
    morally loose; lewd; dissolute; indecent
        adv. licentiously
        noun licentiousness
            The licentious queen brought shame to her country.


307. **libertine** noun (lib′ər-tēn)
    a morally loose person
        noun libertinism
            One must be a libertine to perform in blue movies.


308. **wanton** adj. (won′tən)
    1. morally loose
    2. malicious
    3. not restrained; excessive
        adv. wantonly
        noun wantonness
            Wanton excapades (flings) caused many embarrassments for his family.

309. **prurient** adj. (proͦor′ē-ənt)
    lewd; impure in thought
      adv. pruriently
      noun prurience
      noun pruriency
        The material was written to arouse one's
        prurient interests.

310. **salacious** adj. (sə-lā′shəs)
    lewd; obscene; lustful
      adv. salaciously
      noun salaciousness
      noun salacity
        Sandblasting was used to erase salacious
        graffiti (writings) on the walls of the brick
        building.

311. **profligate** adj. (prof′lə-git)
    1. morally loose
    2. recklessly extravagant
      adv. profligately
      noun profligateness
      noun profligate—a morally loose person; a
                   recklessly extravagant per-
                   son
      noun profligacy
        Profligate gamblers may not get through
        the pearly gates.

312. **didactic** adj (dī-dak′tik)
    instructive; inclined to teach
      adj. didactical
      adv. didactically
      noun didacticism
        The boys didn't like the didactic scout
        leader, but the parents did.

313. **pedantic** adj. (pi-dan′tik)
    excessive show of learning
      adv. pedantically
      noun pedant
      noun pedantry
        Now that your vocabulary has been sig-
        nificantly enhanced (increased), avoid
        being pedantic.

314. **edifying** adj. (ed′ə-fi′ing)
    instructive; enlightening
      adv. edifyingly
      noun edifier
      noun edification
      verb edify—to enlighten; to instruct
        The European trip was an edifying experi-
        ence

315. **pendent** adj. (pen′dənt)
    hanging; suspended
      adv. pendently
      noun pendent—(also spelled pendant) some-
             thing that hangs
        Would you prefer pendent, bracelet or
        pin-on jewelry?

316. **epistle** noun (i-pis′əl)
    a long formal letter
        adj. epistolary
        noun epistler
            The secretary typed a comprehensive epistle.

317. **vexatious** adj. (vek-sā′shəs)
    annoying; irritating
        adj. vexed—irritated; annoyed
        adv. vexatiously
        adv. vexedly
        noun vexatiousness
        noun vexedness
        noun vexation—irritation
        noun vexer
        verb vex—to annoy
            What could be more vexatious than leaving late for an important event and discovering your car has a dead battery?

318. **banal** adj. (bā′nəl)
    ordinary; common because of frequent use
        adv. banally
        noun banality (bə-nal′ə-tē)
            Banal utterances are those heard repeatedly.

319. **trite** adj. (trīt)
    ordinary; common because of frequent use
        adv. tritely
        noun triteness
            Most of us have heard trite statements otherwise they wouldn't be trite.

320. **hackneyed** adj. (hak′nēd)
ordinary; common because of frequent use; stale
Forget the hackneyed expressions and say
something original.


321. **platitude** noun (plat′ə-tōōd)
1. a dull or commonplace statement
2. dullness; triteness
   adj. platitudinous
   verb platitudinize—to utter platitudes
   The speaker who utters one platitude after
   another soon finds himself addressing
   empty chairs.


322. **paltry** adj. (pôl′trē)
almost worthless; trivial
adv. paltrily
noun paltriness
The shrewd investor paid the widow a paltry sum for her valuable antiques.


323. **picayune** adj. (pik′i-yōōn′)
almost worthless
adj. picayunish
noun—picayune—anything of small value
A picayune dollar value was placed on the
antiquated (old) machinery.

324. **impudent** adj. (im′pyə-dənt)
    shameless; offensively bold; rude
    adv. impudently
    noun impudicity
    noun impudence
    noun impudency
        It is not prudent (wise) to be impudent.


325. **impertinent** adj (im-pûr′tə-nənt)
    shameless; offensively bold; disrespectful
    adv. impertinently
    noun impertinence
    noun impertinency
        An impertinent person is an intolerable person.


326. **insolent** adj. (in′sə-lənt)
    shameless; offensively bold; disrespectful
    adv. insolently
    noun insolence
        The insolent pupil was paddled.


327. **effrontery** noun (i-frun′tər-ē)
    shamelessness; offensive boldness
    disrespectfulness
        Don't let effrontery be a part of your personality.

328. **audacious** adj. (ô-dā′shəs)
     shameless; bold
         adv. audaciously
         noun audaciousness
         noun audacity
             The audacious salesman never took no as
             an answer.


329. **presumptuous** adj. (pri-zump′chōō-əs)
     1. shamless; bold
     2. taking too much for granted
         adv. presumptuously
         noun presumptuousness
             Some weather progosticators (predictors)
             have been embarrassed by making pre-
             sumptuous forecasts.


330. **presumptive** adj. (pri-zump′tiv)
     presumed to be, but not proven
         adv. presumptively
             The presumptive murderer was transferred
             to another jail pending (while awaiting) the
             trial.


331. **trenchant** adj. (tren′chənt)
     keen; sharp
         adv. trenchantly
         noun trenchancy
             With trenchant wit, the comedian pre-
             sented one of the funniest performances of
             the evening.

332. **poignant** adj. (poin'yənt)
    1. painful to the feelings
    2. keen; sharp
    adv. poignantly
    noun poignancy
        The convicted public official is still receiving poignant sarcasm.


333. **pungent** adj. (pun'jənt)
    keen; sharp to taste or smell
    adv. pungently
    noun pungency
    noun pungence
        The pungent odor of burning rubber rolled from the smoke stacks.


334. **piquant** adj. (pē'kənt, pē'kwənt)
    1. agreeably sharp; tart
    2. lively and charming; interesting
    adv. piquantly
    noun piquancy
        The connoisseur enjoyed a piquant sauce on his seafood.


335. **privy** adj. (priv'ē)
    privately or secretly aware (used with to)
    adv. privily
    noun privity
        Only a few people were privy to the transaction.

336. **reconnoiter** verb (rē′kə-noi′tər)
    to examine; to survey
        noun reconnoiterer
        noun reconnoissance—a survey
        A special division will reconnoiter the area
        for enemy activity.

337. **demeanor** noun (di-mē′nər)
    behavior; conduct
        The imposter's demeanor was realistic.

338. **comport** verb (kəm-pōrt′)
    1. to conduct (oneself); to behave
    2. to agree—comport in this case is followed by
            with (comport with a decision)
        noun comportment—behavior
        In church we comport ourselves diffe-
        rently than we do outside.

339. **countenance** noun (koun′tə-nəns)
    1. facial expression; appearance
    2. approval
    3. self-control; composure
        The young president handled the angry
        stockholders with the countenance of a
        concerned and sympathetic man.

340. **decorous** adj. (dek′ər-əs)
    proper
        adv. decorously
        noun decorousness
        noun decorum
        Decorous behavior is not a characteristic
        of a lout (rude person).

341. **posture** noun (pos′chər)
   1. a mental attitude; a frame of mind
   2. the position of the body
      adj. postural
      noun posturer
      noun posturist
      verb posturize—to pose
         He has the posture to someday be a minister.

342. **seemly** adj. (sēm′lē)
   proper
      noun seemliness
         The consistent and seemly behavior of a leader dog is important.

343. **impropriety** noun (im′prə-prī′ə-tē)
   an improper action; incorrectness;
   improper conduct
         The impropriety of the official disgusted his constituents (followers).

344. **seeming** adj. (sē′ming)
   apparently true, but not necessarily
      adv. seemingly
      noun seemingness
         His huge and muscular body gave the wrestler a seeming advantage over his much smaller opponent.

345. **seamy** adj. (sē′mē)
    unpleasant; sordid
        noun seaminess
            The tour showed the seamy side of slum life.

346. **disposition** noun (dis′pə-zish′ən)
    a mental or physical inclination
        A person with a happy disposition is pleasant company.

347. **disposed** adj. (dis-pōzd′)
    inclined
        Being disposed to alcohol is unhealthy.

348. **prodigal** adj. (prod′ə-gəl)
    wasteful
        noun prodigal—one who is wasteful
            Prodigal expenditures were made testing the new product.

349. **wastrel** noun (wās′trəl)
    a spendthrift; a waster
        Money is something the worker earns and the wastrel burns.

350. **objurgate** verb (ob′jər-gāt)
    to scold; to blame
        adj. objurgatory
        adv. objurgatorily
        noun objurgation
        noun objurgator
            Expect the teacher to objurgate you if you are caught cheating.

351. **upbraid** verb (up-brād′)
    to scold; to blame
      adv. upbraidingly
      noun upbraiding
      noun upbraider
         The unhappy customer was ready to up-braid the clerk for defective merchandise.

352. **reprehend** verb (rep′ri-hend′)
    to scold; to blame; to criticize severely
         Courts reprehend and incarcerate (jail) the guilty.

353. **rebuke** verb (ri-bȳook′)
    to scold; to blame
      adj. rebukable
      noun rebuker
      noun rebuke—a scolding; a reprimand
         A teacher is expected to rebuke a loquacious (talkative) class.

354. **reprimand** verb (rep′rə-mand)
    to scold; to blame
      noun reprimand—a severe scolding
         The student said, "Don't reprimand me; I didn't do it."

355. **reprove** verb (ri'pro͞ov')
   to scold; to blame
   adj. reprovable
   adv. reprovingly
   noun reprover
   News commentators often reprove politi-
   cians for unseemly (improper) conduct.

356. **reproach** verb (ri-prōch')
   to scold; to blame
   adj. reproachable
   adv. reproachably
   noun reproachableness
   noun reproacher
   noun reproach—the act of reproaching; dis-
                   grace
   They had better have the facts correct if
   they expect to reproach the official
   publicly.

357. **reproachful** adj. (ri-prōch'fəl)
   expressing blame or reproach
   adv. reproachfully
   noun reproachfulness
   Indiscriminate killing of wildlife will generate unkind words from reproachful en-
   vironmentalists.

358. **reproof** noun (ri-pro͞of')
   the act of scolding, blaming, rebuking, censuring
   or reproving
   Oil drillers try to avoid reproof from
   ecological organizations.

359. **culpable** adj. (kul′pə-bəl)
    deserving blame
      adv. culpably
      noun culpability
      noun culpableness
        Culpable schemes were used by the winning team.

360. **reprehensible** adj. (rep′ri-hen′sə-bəl)
    deserving blame
      adv. reprehensibly
      noun reprehensibility
      noun reprehensibleness
        The vociferous (noisy) group felt the Viet-Nam involvement was reprehensible.

361. **rebuff** verb (ri-buf′)
    to reject; to repel
      noun rebuff—a refusal; a snub
        She'll rebuff any marital proposals.

362. **rebut** verb (ri-but′)
    to refute by evidence
      noun rebuttal
      noun rebutter
        The debater tried to rebut the argument of his opponent with documented information.

363. **refute** verb (ri-fyo͞ot′)
to prove that a statement, opinion, charge, etc. is incorrect or false
adj. refutable
adv. refutably
noun refutability
noun refutal
noun refuter
noun refutation—disproof
It is hard to refute a statement based on solid evidence and fact.


364. **obtrusive** adj. (əb-tro͞o′siv)
very forward; forcing oneself or opinion upon another uninvitedly
adv. obtrusively
noun obtrusiveness
noun obtrusion
noun obtruder
verb obtrude—to force oneself upon another
She wouldn't date him because of his obtrusive ways.


365. **officious** adj. (ə-fish′əs)
very forward; forcing oneself or opinion upon another
adv. officiously
noun officiousness
The officious interference was unappreciated.

366. **intrusive** adj. (in-trōō′siv)
   very forward; forcing oneself or opinion upon
   another uninvitedly
     adv. intrusively
     noun intrusiveness
     noun intrusion
     noun intruder
     verb intrude
       Intrusive manners don't win friendships.

367. **encroach** verb (in-krōch′)
   to intrude; to advance beyond proper limits; to
   trespass
     noun encroacher
     noun encroachment
       If you encroach upon his private estate,
       you're liable to be arrested.

368. **inroad** noun (in′rōd′)
   a harmful trespass; a serious encroachment
       Prodigal (wasteful) expenditures can make
       serious inroads (usually plural) on one's sav-
       ings account.

369. **servile** adj. (sûr′vĭl)
   like a slave (obedient, submissive, obsequious,
   sycophantic)
     adv. servilely
     noun servility
     noun servileness
     noun servitor—a servant
       Some employers demand servile loyalty
       from their employees.

370. **obsequious** adj. (əb-sē′kwē-əs)

excessively obedient or submissive; extremely servile or sycophantic

adv. obsequiously

noun obsequiousness

The obsequious waitress eventually became quite obnoxious.


371. **sycophant** noun (sik′ə-fənt)

an insincere servile flatterer; a servile person

adj. sycophantic

adj. sycophantantical

adv. sycophantically

noun sycophancy

The sycophant, hovering continuously near the off-key singer of the band, praised his singing abilities.


372. **toady** noun (tō′dē)

an insincere servile flatterer (more repulsive than a sycophant); a servile person

adj. toadyish

noun toadyism

verb toady—to flatter for favors

The toady gave much attention to the old millionaire in hopes of being made part of his will.

373. **subservient** adj. (səb-sûr′vē-ənt)
   of inferior capacity; like a slave
      adv. subserviently
      noun subservientness
      noun subservience
      noun subserviency
      noun subservient—one who subserves
      verb subserve—to serve as a subordinate to
            another
         The chauffeur was fired for not de-
         monstrating subservient behavior.


374. **deferential** adj. (def′ə-ren′shəl)
   respectful; courteous
      adj. deferent
      adv. deferentially
      noun deference
         The undertaker talked in deferential tones
         to the family of the deceased.


375. **reverent** adj. (rev′ər-ənt)
   respectful
      adj. reverential
      adv. reverently
      adv. reverentially
      noun reverence
      verb revere—to respect
         All good people should have reverent re-
         gards for their fellow man.

376. **venerable** adj. (ven′ər-ə-bəl)
     deserving repect
        adv. venerably
        noun venerability
        noun venerableness
        noun veneration—a feeling of deep respect;
                                reverence
        verb venerate—to respect
           Venerable institutions include churches
           and court houses.

377. **deplete** verb (di-plēt′)
     to exhaust; to reduce
        adj. depletive—causing depletion
        adj. depletory
        noun depletion
           Solar energy may be another source of
           power after we deplete our petroleum re-
           sources.

378. **delete** verb (di-lēt′)
     to cancel; to take out
        noun deletion
           The treasurer suggested that club members
           delete all unnecessary expenses from the
           budget.

379. **obviate** verb (ob′vē-āt)
     to make unnecessary; to remove
        noun obviation
        noun obviator
           A will should obviate lengthy probate court
           proceedings.

131

380. **preclude** verb (pri-klo͞od′)

>to prevent; to shut out; to make impossible; to eliminate
>>adj. preclusive
>>adv. preclusively
>>noun preclusion
>>>The new law will preclude the sale of throw-away bottles after the first of the year.

381. **rescind** verb (ri-sind′)

>to cancel; to repeal; to abrogate
>>adj. rescindable
>>adj. rescissible
>>noun rescinder
>>noun rescission
>>>The president had to rescind the program because of public resentment.

382. **abrogate** verb (ab′rə-gāt)

>to abolish; to rescind; to repeal
>>adj. abrogable
>>adj. abrogative
>>noun abrogation
>>noun abrogator
>>>The legislature may soon abrogate the death penalty law.

383. **expunge** verb (ik-spunj′)

>to strike out; to delete; to erase; to wipe out
>>noun expunction
>>noun expunger
>>>A doctor's note will expunge the tardiness from your record.

384. **negate** verb (nē'gāt)
   1. to deny; to contradict
   2. to nullify; to make ineffective
   adj. negational
   adj. negatory
   noun negation
   > The sudden change for the better, in the weather, will negate cancellation of the trip.

385. **nullify** verb (nul'ə-fī)
   to annul; to make ineffective; to make useless
   noun nullification
   noun nullificationist
   noun nullifier
   noun nullificator
   > Certainly a judge will nullify such an unreasonable contract.

386. **gratuity** noun (grə-too'ə-tē)
   a gift; a tip
   > A fifteen-percent gratuity was included on the bill.

387. **gratuitous** adj. (grə-too'ə-təs)
   1. uncalled for; unwarranted
   2. given freely; free
   adv. gratuitously
   noun gratuitousness
   noun gratuity—a gift; a tip
   > Gratuitous violence on television is a hotly debated issue.

388. **deleterious** adj. (del'ə-tir'ē-əs)
   harmful; injurious; hurtful to health or morals;
   noxious
      adv. deleteriously
      noun deleteriousness
        If consumed, spoiled food may be dele-
        terious to one's health.

389. **noxious** adj. (nok'shəs)
   harmful; injurious; hurtful to health or morals;
   deleterious
      adv. noxiously
      noun noxiousness
        Can movies loaded with killing and stealing
        be noxious to our country's morals?

390. **injurious** adj. (in-jŏŏr'ē-əs)
   harmful; hurtful; detrimental
      adv. injuriously
      noun injuriousness
      verb injure—to hurt
        Smoking is an injurious habit.

391. **nocuous** adj. (nok'yŏŏ-əs)
   harmful; hurtful; detrimental; injurious
      adv. nocuously
      noun nocuousness
        Getting sprayed by an excited skunk is not
        nocuous, just smelly.

392. **noisome** adj. (noi′səm)
   1. harmful; injurious; noxious
   2. offensive or disgustinging in smell; stinking
      adv. noisomely
      noun noisomeness
        Noisome smoke rolled from the foundry's chimney.

393. **pernicious** adj. (pər-nish′əs)
   extremely harmful; extremely injurious; extremely hurtful; deadly
      adv. perniciously
      noun perniciousness
        The snake handler received a pernicious bite.

394. **baneful** adj. (bān′fəl)
   extremely harmful; poisonous; pernicious
      adv. banefully
      noun banefulness
        Mushroom hunters should learn the baneful species.

395. **delectable** adj. (di-lek′tə-bəl)
   delightful; enjoyable
      adv. delectably
      noun delectableness
      noun delectability
      noun delectation—a delight; enjoyment
      verb delectate—to delight; to charm
        Many guests thanked the hostess for the delectable evening.

396. **savory** adj. (sā′vər-ē)
    pleasing to taste or smell
        adv. savorily
        noun savoriness
            A savory meal of wild game was served at
            the sportsmen's banquet.

397. **sapid** adj. (sap′id)
    1. tasty
    2. interesting; to one's liking
        noun sapidity
        noun sapidness
            The exotic food was extremely sapid.

398. **palatable** adj. (pal′it-ə-bəl)
    1. pleasing to the taste
    2. agreeable; acceptable
        adv. palatably
        noun palatability
        noun palatableness
            Ambrosia, the palatable food of the gods in
            classical mythology, was said to give
            immortality.

399. **cuisine** noun (kwi-zēn′)
    a style of cooking
        Yes, Tony prefers Italian cuisine.

400. **fastidious** adj. (fas-tid′ē-əs)
    hard to please; persnickety; fussy
        adv. fastidiously
        noun fastidiousness
            A fastidious shopper left the clothes rack a
            mixed-up mess.

**Test 4**

1. abrogate  a. rescind  b. restrict  c. appeal
   d. detest
2. audacious  a. noisy  b. bold  c. pleasant
   sounding  d. particular
3. banal  a. ordinary  b. flat  c. edible  d. stupid
4. baneful  a. trivial  b. noticeable  c. often
   d. poisonous
5. comport  a. exaggerate  b. disagree  c. berate
   d. conduct
6. countenance  a. appearance  b. royalty
   c. meaning  d. illustration
7. cuisine  a. congreation  b. heavy eater
   c. dunce  d. style of cooking
8. culpable  a. deserving respect  b. useful
   c. deserving blame  d. suspicious
9. decorous  a. proper  b. shameless
   c. preposterous  d. delicious
10. deferential  a. unusual  b. agonizing
    c. standard  d. courteous
11. delectable  a. enjoyable  b. peculiar
    c. erasable  d. colloquial
12. delete  a. rise  b. educate  c. refer  d. cancel
13. deleterious  a. vulgar  b. continuous
    c. unnatural  d. harmful
14. demeanor  a. source  b. behavior  c. dignity
    meanness
15. deplete  a. exhaust  b. complain  c. rehearse
    d. record
16. didactic  a. forceful  b. appropriate  c. creative
    d. instructive
17. disposed  a. sufficient  b. inclined  c. notable
    d. unhealthy

137

18. disposition a. inclination b. unhealthiness
    c. meaningfulness d. happiness
19. dissolute a. prudish b. morally loose c. poor
    d. idealistic
20. edifying a. enlightening b. hungry c. greedy
    d. random
21. effrontery a. strangeness b. building face
    c. boldness d. usage
22. encroach a. shoot b. move c. trespass
    d. retreat
23. epistle a. gravestone b. instrument c. letter
    d. book
24. expunge a. translate b. express c. convey
    d. erase
25. fastidious a. previous b. accelerated c. fussy
    d. zany
26. gratuitous a. welcomed b. unwarranted
    c. frequent d. costly
27. gratuity a. congratulation b. tip c. distortion
    c. hilarity
28. hackneyed a. ordinary b. freakish c. sick
    d. downtrodden
29. impertinent a. disrespectful b. unrelated
    c. true d. not caring
30. impropriety a. submission b. ownership
    c. motion d. incorrectness
31. impudent a. bold b. unproductive c. natural
    d. reverent
32. injurious a. habitual b. sickly c. harmful
    d. incapable
33. inroad a. end b. trespass c. extensiveness
    d. journey

34. insolent  a. shameless  b. respectful
    c. well-bred  d. razor sharp
35. intrusive  a. honorable  b. indescribable
    c. forward  d. comparative
36. inveigh  a. call for help  b. warn
    c. attack with words  d. scream
37. lascivious  a. lewd  b. blond  d. twisting
    d. self-motivated
38. libertine a. freedom b. morally
    inhibited person c. morally loose person
    d. decadence
39. libidinous  a. preventable  b. lustful
    c. objectionable  d. fashionable
40. licentious  a. poetic  b. indecent  c hampering
    d. musically
41. lustful  a. super sensitive  b. restrained
    c. liberated  d. driven by sexual desire
42. negate  a. murder  b. preserve
    c. make productive  d. make ineffective
43. nocuous  a. regular  b. nonsensical  c. harmful
    d. evil looking
44. noisome  a. new  b. unbearable  c. stinking
    d. obnoxiously noisy
45. noxious  a. zigzag  b. unbearable  c. disgusting
    d. harmful
46. nullify  a. postpone  b. forget  c. annul
    d. make one look foolish
47. objurgate  a. bail out  b. gamble  c. order
    d. scold
48. obsequious  a. plump  b. like a slave
    c. imprisoned  d. inaudible
49. obtrusive  a. very forward  b. depressed
    c. requiring extreme effort  d. faint

50. obviate  a. make unnecessary  b. move
    c. create disturbance  d. energize
51. officious  a. forward  b. argumentive
    c. definitive  d. important
52. palatable  a. obvious  b. agreeable
    c. beneficial  d. vivid
53. paltry  a. trivial  b. highly thought of
    c. shrewd  d. valuable
54. pedantic  a. many sided figure  b. suspended
    c. projecting  d. excessive show of learning
55. pendent  a. simple  b. inclined  c. suspended
    d. fancy
56. pernicious  a. extremely frugal  b. direct
    c. extremely harmful  d. demanding
57. picayune  a. worthless  b. memorable  c. lucid
    d. ornate
58. piquant  a. unadorned  b. agreeably sharp
    c. hindering  d. salty
59. platitude  a. excitement  b. dullness
    c. sufficiency  d. carefulness
60. poignant  a. volatile  b. fragile  c. keen
    d. cheerless

61. posture  a. wisdom  b. wickedness  c. mischief
    d. mental attitude
62. preclude  a. toil  b. abide  c. uncover
    d. prevent
63. presumptive  a. amiss  b. accurate  c. polished
    d. presumed
64. presumptuous  a. ornate  b. elaborate
    c. shameless  d. generous
65. privy  a. secretly aware  b. openhanded
    c. fictitous  d. good tempered

66. prodigal  a. heavy  b. wasteful  c. juvenile
    d. decrepit
67. profligate  a. conclusive  b. earsplitting
    c. instructive  d. morally loose
68. prurient  a. impure in thought  b. thoughtless
    c. feeble  d. strangely different
69. pungent  a. warm to touch  b. rested  c. pert
    d. sharp to taste
70. rebuff  a. reject  b. polish  c. withdraw  d. slow
    down
71. rebuke  a. injure  b. scold  c. dismiss
    d. do over
72. rebut  a. quell  b. desert  c. refute
    d. speak loudly
73. reconnoiter  a. deal with  b. jabber  c. inform
    d. examine
74. refute  a. to prove incorrect  b. refuse  c. give
    away  d. deliver
75. reprehend  a. subdue  b. caution  c. blame
    d. contradict
76. reprehensible  a. controversial  b. submissive
    c. blameworthy  d. ill-favored
77. reprimand  a. heed  b. repeat  c. repell  d. scold
78. reproach  a. trespass  b. blame
    c. do over again  d. please
79. reproachful  a. expressing love
    b. expressing blame  c. expressing concern
    d. harmful
80. reproof  a. act of scolding  b. act of restricting
    c. remoteness  d. procedure
81. reprove  a. consult  b. tickle  c. convince
    d. scold

82. rescind  a. return  b. cancel  c. denote
    d. give away
83. reverent  a. applicable  b. respectful
    c. rambling  d. reversible
84. salacious  a. lengthy  b. flighty  c. obscene
    d. soothing
85. sapid  a. dull  b. slow  c. empty  d. tasty
86. savory  a. carefully planned
    b. pleasing to taste  c. personable  d. watery
87. seamy  a. clean  b. deeply rooted
    c. unpleasant  d. proper
88. seeming  a. extremely hot  b. apparently true
    c. undignified  d. great
89. seemly  a. aimless  b. physical  c. tottery
    d. proper
90. servile  a. obedient  b. employable
    c. purposeless  d. classy
91. subservient  a. of superior quality
    b. of inferior capacity  c. aging
    d. underground
92. sycophant  a. righteous person  b. sick person
    c. largeness  d. servile person
93. toady  a. jumpy person  b. insincere servile
    flatterer  c. amphibian  d. senility
94. trenchant  a. sliced  b. timeworn  c. keen
    d. passé
95. trite  a. unusual  b. cute  c. slick  d. ordinary
96. upbraid  a. blame  b. tie up  c. analyze
    d. comment critically
97. venerable  a. deserving respect
    b. deserving blame  c. intensive
    d. magnificent

98. vexatious  a. scarce  b. foxy  c. bullish
    d. annoying
99. wanton  a. desireous  b. weak  c. unbroken
    d. excessive
100. wastrel  a. trash container  b. spendthrift
    c. positive approach  d. loser

## Test 4

### Answers

| | | | |
|---|---|---|---|
| 1. a | 26. b | 51. a | 76. c |
| 2. b | 27. b | 52. b | 77. d |
| 3. a | 28. a | 53. a | 78. b |
| 4. d | 29. a | 54. d | 79. b |
| 5. d | 30. d | 55. c | 80. a |
| 6. a | 31. a | 56. c | 81. d |
| 7. d | 32. c | 57. a | 82. b |
| 8. c | 33. b | 58. b | 83. b |
| 9. a | 34. a | 59. b | 84. c |
| 10. d | 35. c | 60. c | 85. d |
| 11. a | 36. c | 61. d | 86. b |
| 12. d | 37. a | 62. d | 87. c |
| 13. d | 38. c | 63. d | 88. b |
| 14. b | 39. b | 64. c | 89. d |
| 15. a | 40. b | 65. a | 90. a |
| 16. d | 41. d | 66. b | 91. b |
| 17. b | 42. d | 67. d | 92. d |
| 18. a | 43. c | 68. a | 93. b |
| 19. b | 44. c | 69. d | 94. c |
| 20. a | 45. d | 70. a | 95. d |
| 21. c | 46. c | 71. b | 96. a |
| 22. c | 47. d | 72. c | 97. a |
| 23. c | 48. b | 73. d | 98. d |
| 24. d | 49. a | 74. a | 99. d |
| 25. c | 50. a | 75. c | 100. b |

## SCORING

Correct answers
- 100-90=A (excellent)
- 89-80=B (good)
- 79-70=C (fair)
- 69-60=D (poor)
- 59- 0=E (Start over!)

Score before word study _____

Score after word study _____

401. **persnickety** adj. (pər-snik′ə-tē)
hard to please; fastidious; fussy
noun persnicketiness
The persnickety eater picked all the shrimp
from the salad.

402. **meticulous** adj. (mə-tik′yə-ləs)
extremely careful about details
adv. meticulously
noun meticulousity
noun meticulousness
Fashion models must be meticulous dres-
sers.

403. **punctilious** adj. (pungk-til′ē-əs)
extremely careful about conduct
adv. punctiliously
noun punctiliousness
The punctilious butler ushered the dig-
nitaries to the dining room.

404. **scrupulous** adj. (skrōō′pyə-ləs)
careful; exact; upright; conscientious
adv. scrupulously
noun scrupulosity
noun scrupulousness
A scrupulous inventory was made at year's
end.

405. **vociferous** adj. (vō-sif′ər-əs)
shouting, characterized by loud voice; noisy; vociferant
  adv. vociferously
  noun vociferousness
    Sitting in front of a vociferous racing enthusiast at the horse race was a pain in the ear.

406. **vociferant** adj, (vō-sif′ər-ənt)
shouting, characterized by loud voice; noisy; vociferous
  noun vociferation
  noun vociferator
  noun vociferance
  noun vociferant—a noisy, shouting person
  verb vociferate—to shout
    The fans became more vociferant when the cheerleaders appeared on the field.

407. **clamorous** adj. (klam′ər-əs)
  1. shouting, characterized by loud voice; vociferous; vociferant
  2. loud and continuously noisy
  adv. clamorously
  noun clamorousness
  noun clamor
  verb clamor—to make loud complaints or demands; to shout; to make noise
    Discothèques are often too clamorous for pleasant conversing.

408. **blatant** adj. (blā′tənt)
1. offensively noisy; obnoxiously loud
2. obvious
adv. blatantly
noun blatancy
Have you ever seen such blatant stupidity in your life?

409. **constituent** noun (kən-stich′ōō-ənt)
1. a voter
2. a component; an important part or element
adj. constituent—serving as a component or part of something
noun constituency
The newly elected mayor paused to thank a constituent.

410. **consternation** noun (kon′stər-nā′shən)
fright; bewilderment; alarm
verb consternate—to terrorize; to alarm
To the consternation of the crew, the ship rolled hard to its starboard (right) side.

411. **eschew** verb (es-chōō′)
to avoid; to shun
noun eschewer
noun eschewal
As you slide down the banister of life may you eschew the splinters that point your way.

412. **circumvent** verb (sûr′kəm-vent′)
to avoid; to go around
adj. circumventive
noun circumvention
noun circumventor or circumventer
Truck drivers must circumvent low bridges.

413. **circuitous** adj. (sər-kyo͞o′ə-təs)
roundabout; not direct
adv. circuitously
noun circuitousness
noun circuity
The soldiers made a circuitous approach on the enemy fort.

414. **circumlocution** noun (sûr′kəm-lō-kyo͞o′shən)
roundabout and indirect expression
adj. circumlocutory
The shrewd lawyer was adept at using circumlocution when answering crucial questions from the press.

415. **incongruous** adj. (in-kong′gro͞o-əs)
out of place; incompatible to the point of being absurd; inappropriate
adj. incongruent
adv. incongruently
adv. incongruously
noun incongruousness
noun incongruity
noun incongruence
Thinking that a team of horses can pull a hydraulic plow is completely incongruous.

416. **proffer** verb (prof´ər)
    to offer
        noun proffer—an offer; act of offering
        noun profferer
            Just before the drop of the hammer, the
            bidder decided to proffer a larger bid.

417. **evitable** adj. (ev´ə-tə-bəl)
    avoidable
        Many highway accidents are evitable.

418. **inevitable** adj. (in-ev´ə-tə-bəl
    unavoidable
        adv. inevitably
        noun inevitability
        noun inevitableness
            Death is inevitable.

419. **permeable** adj. (pûr´mē-ə-bəl)
    allowing passage; capable of being penetrated or
    passed through
        adj. permeant
        adj. permeative
        adv. permeably
        noun permeability
        noun permeance
        noun permeation
        verb permeate—to penetrate
            Grain in the permeable burlap bag was
            spoiled by an unexpected rain storm.

420. **pervasive** adj. (pər-vā′siv)
  spreading; passing through; penetrating; permeating
    adv. pervasively
    noun pervasiveness
    noun pervader
    noun pervasion
    verb pervade—to spread throughout
      The pervasive fragrance of freshly cut flowers filled the room.

421. **divergent** adj. (di-vûr′jənt)
  different; deviating
    adv. divergently
    noun divergence
    noun divergency
    verb diverge
      Members of the planning commission had divergent ideas on rezoning proposals.

422. **confection** noun (kən-fek′shən)
  a candy; a sweet preparation
    adj confectionary—pertaining to confections
    noun confectioner—one who deals in confections
    noun confectionery—a candy shop; candies collectively
      Excuse me, where is the closest confectionery? I'd like to buy some confection.

423. **rueful** adj. (rōō′fəl)
   deplorable; pitiable; regretful; dejected
   adv. ruefully
   noun ruefullness
   verb rue—to feel sorrow
   Let us all be concerned with the rueful plight (condition) of our poor and aged citizens.

424. **remorseful** adj. (ri-môrs′fəl)
   full of deep regret; deep feeling of grief or distress due to sense of guilt
   adv. remorsefully
   noun remorsefulness
   noun remorse
   The driver was in a remorseful mood after hitting the bicyclist.

425. **compunctious** adj. (kəm-pungk′shəs)
   uneasiness of feeling; regretful; slight feeling of grief or distress due to sense of guilt
   adv. compunctiously
   noun compunction
   He had no compunctious feelings about skipping school.

426. **semblance** noun (sem′bləns)
   1. an outward appearance
   2. a likeness
   The patient had the semblance of an individual under great pressure.

152

427. **superficial** adj. (soo′pər-fish′əl)
being on or near the surface
adj. superficiary
adv. superficially
noun superficialness
noun superficiality
A superficial cut is usually treated with
antiseptic and a bandage.

428. **jocund** adj. (jō′kənd)
cheerful; glad; jovial
adv. jocundly
noun jocundity
noun jocundness
When the stock market spurted upward,
the jocund broker held a celebration party.

429. **levity** noun (lev′ə-tē)
lack of seriousness; lightness
The proper use of levity can be a valuable
tool for the public speaker.

430. **jocular** adj. (jok′yə-lər)
humorous; making jokes
adj. joculatory
adv. jocularly
noun jocularity
An otherwise boring lecture was made tolerable
by the professor's jocular comments.

431. **jocose** adj. (jō-kōs′)
   humorous; making jokes
      adv. jocosely
      noun jocoseness
      noun jocosity
         The jocose luncheon conversation with the usually sedate (reserved) boss surprised the employee.

432. **waggish** adj. (wag′ish)
   humorous; making jokes
      adv. waggishly
      noun waggishness
      noun waggery—a joke
      noun wag—a joker
         The ridiculous question received an appropriately waggish reply.

433. **facetious** adj. (fə-sē′shəs)
   humorous; making jokes
      adv. facetiously
      noun facetiousness
         Her homemade newspaper dress provoked many facetious remarks.

434. **flippant** adj. (flip′ənt)
   1. disrespectful; smart in speech
   2. lacking seriousness
      adv. flippantly
      noun flippancy
      noun flippantness
         The flippant student was suspended.

435. **jesting** adj. (jes′ting)
   lacking seriousness; playful
   adv. jestingly
   noun jest—a joke
   noun jester
   noun jesting—playfulness
   verb jest—to joke
   During a tense moment, the negotiator's jesting approach eased heightened emotions.

436. **ribald** adj. (rib′əld)
   vulgar or offensive joking
   noun ribaldry
   Refrain from telling ribald jokes in mixed company!

437. **buffoon** noun (bu-fo͞on′)
   a clown; a joker
   adj. buffoonish
   noun buffoonery—tricks and pranks
   A big buffoon skipped around the arena followed by a small dog wearing a buffoonish costume.

438. **jejune** adj. (jə-jo͞on′)
   1. dull; uninteresting; insipid
   2. lacking in nourishment
   adv. jejunely
   noun jejuneness
   noun jejunity
   A vacation not properly planned may turn into a jejune experience.

439. **vapid** adj. (vap′id)
   dull; insipid; no liveliness
   adv. vapidly
   noun vapidity
   noun vapidness
   Finding the program vapid, he turned to another channel.


440. **insipid** adj. (in-sip′id)
   dull; uninteresting
   adv. insipidly
   noun insipidness
   noun insipidity
   Many students find history books insipid reading.


441. **prosaic** adj. (prō-zā′ik)
   dull; uninteresting; ordinary
   adj. prosaical
   adv. prosaically
   noun prosaicness
   The candidate's platform was too prosaic to sway many voters.


442. **perfunctory** adj. (pər-fungk′tər-ē)
   done mechanically and without enthusiasm; mechanical; indifferent
   adv. perfunctorily
   noun perfunctoriness
   The car assembler had the perfunctory task of putting two bolts in each bumper.

443. **deify** verb (dē′ə-fī)
    to worship; to glorify
        adj. deific—(dē-if′ik)—divine
        adj. deifical
        noun deification
        noun deifier
            Some people deify money, thus demonstrating warped values.

444. **propitious** adj. (prō-pish′əs)
    1. favorable; auspicious; advantageous
    2. kindly; gracious; favorably inclined (propitious may also be used to describe people whereas auspicious may not)
        adv. propitiously
        noun propitiousness
        verb propitiate—to make favorable; to conciliate; to appease
    Propitious weather is once again predicted.

445. **auspicious** adj. (ôs-pish′əs)
    favorable
        adv. auspiciously
        noun auspiciousness
            The runner got off to an auspicious start, but an unfortunate stumble cost him the race.

446. **auspices** noun (ôs′pə-sēz)
    guidance
            The music student studied under the auspices of a renowned (famous) composer.

447. **tutelage** noun (to͞o′tə-lij)
> guidance; training; guardianship
>> adj. tutelary
>>> Under the tutelage of an expert mechanic he learned enough to open his own repair shop.

448. **pedagogue** noun (ped′ə-gog)
> a teacher
>> adj. pedagogic
>> adj. pedagogical
>> adv. pedagogically
>> noun pedagogism
>> noun pedagogy
>>> English class had a substitute pedagogue for three days.

449. **anachronism** noun (ə-nak′rə-niz′əm)
> a person, event, or thing out of its proper time period
>> adj anachronistic
>> adj. anachronistical
>> adj. anachronous
>> adv. anachronously
>>> The use of an electric can opener in a western movie would be an anachronism.

450. **edacity** noun (i-das′ə-tē)
> the act of eating excessively; the act of gluttony
>> adj. edacious
>> adv. edaciously
>>> He's guilty of edacity every Thanksgiving.

451. **gluttony** noun (glut′n-ē)
   the act of eating excessively; the act of edacity
   adj. gluttonous
   adv. gluttonously
   noun gluttonousness
   noun glutton
   verb gluttonize—to eat like a glutton
      The anticipation of gluttony is delightful
      but the consequences are upsetting.


452. **voracious** adj. (vô-rā′shəs)
   greedy; consuming in great quantities
   adv. voraciously
   noun voracity
   noun voraciousness
      Snarling hyenas with voracious appetites
      devoured the carcass in minutes.


453. **rapacious** adj. (rə-pā′shəs)
   greedy; grasping
   adv. rapaciously
   noun rapacity
   noun rapaciousness
      The rapacious reader had several books at
      his bedside.


454. **cupidity** noun (kyōō-pid′ə-tē)
   greed; avarice
      Cupidity should not be one's motivation.

455. **avarice** noun (av′ə-ris)
    greed; cupidity
        adj. avaricious
        adv. avariciously
        noun avariciousness
            Fairy tales are often centered around kings
            obsessed with avarice.

456. **covetous** adj. (kuv′ə-təs)
    greedy; desirous
        adv. covetously
        noun covetousness
        noun coveter
        verb covet—to desire; to want
            The Bible tells us no man should be covet-
            ous of another's wife.

457. **omnivorous** adj. (om-niv′ər-əs)
    devouring everything
        adv. omnivorously
        noun omnivorousness
            An omnivorous eater eats everything and
            anything.

458. **insatiable** adj. (ɪn-sā'shə-bəl)
    extremely greedy; incapable of being satisfied
      adj. insatiate
      adv. insatiably
      adv. insatiately
      noun insatiability
      noun insatiableness
      noun insatiateness
        Even though a millionaire, he had an insatiable lust (strong desire) for additional wealth.

459. **satiate** verb (sā'shē-āt)
    to fill beyond natural desire; to glut; to surfeit
      adj. satiable
      adv. satiably
      noun satiability—the state of being overly gratified
      noun satiableness
      noun satiation
        "Don't satiate yourselves before dessert," warned the hostess.

460. **surfeit** verb (sûr'fit)
    to fill beyond natural desire; to glut; to satiate
      noun surfeit—the act of filling to excess; the state of being excessively full
      noun surfeiter
        A week of T.V. horror films might surfeit viewers to the point that they switch to other programming.

461. **replete** adj. (ri-plēt′)
    filled; abounding
        noun repleteness
        noun repletion
            The collector had a house replete with antiques from around the world.

462. **fraught** adj. (frôt)
    filled (usually followed by with)
        The canoe trip is fraught with danger.

463. **fruition** noun (frōō-ish′ən)
    completion; the realization of something worked for; fulfillment
        He'd like to see his dream house reach fruition, but he is out of money.

464. **efflorescent** adj. (ef′lôr-es′ənt)
    blossoming; blooming
        noun efflorescence
        verb effloresce
            Efflorescent lilies make nice Easter gifts.

465. **exotic** adj. (ig-zot′ik)
    foreign; strangely different
        adv. exotically
        noun exoticism
        noun exotic—something foreign
            Hundreds of exotic flowers and plants were exhibited at the garden show.

466. **erotic** adj. (i-rot′ik)
   pertaining to sensual love
   adv. erotically
   noun eroticism
   noun erotica (plural)—erotic pictures, books,
   etc.
   Many film stories are built around an erotic
   affair.

467. **garrulous** adj. (gar′ə-ləs) or (gar′yə-ləs)
   talkative; loquacious
   adv. garrulously
   noun garrulousness
   noun garrulity
   The garrulous salesman persisted with his
   spiel (high pressured sales talk) despite the
   customer's obvious lack of interest.

468. **loquacious** adj. (lō-kwā′shəs)
   talkative
   adv. loquaciously
   noun loquacity
   noun loquaciousness
   The loquacious students were given extra
   homework.

469. **prattle** noun (prat′l)
   foolish talk; childish speech
   noun prattler
   verb prattle—to talk foolishly
   Baby talk is a good example of prattle.

470. **flapdoodle** noun (flap'dood'l)
    foolish talk
        The teacher told her class to cut the flap-
        doodle and begin the lesson.


471. **twaddle** noun (twod'l)
    foolish talk
        noun twaddler
        verb twaddle—to talk foolishly
        The teenage girls were engrossed in twad-
        dle as they stood in the theater line.


472. **palaver** noun (pə-lav'ər)
    1. idle talk
    2. a discussion
        noun palaverer
        verb palaver—to talk idly
        Bored by the palaver of her roommate, she
        went for a walk.


473. **glib** adj. (glib)
    fluent, but thoughtless and insincere
        adv. glibly
        noun glibness
        He compliments with a glib tongue.


474. **parlance** noun (pär'ləns)
    language; manner of speech
        The lawyer converted the oral purchase
        offer into binding legal parlance.


164

475. **complacent** ad. (kəm-plā′sənt)
self-satisfied; pleased
adv. complacently
noun complacency
noun complacence
With a complacent look, the painter ad-
mired his new creation.

476. **complaisant** adj. (kəm-plā′zənt)
desiring to please; yielding; compliant
adv. complaisantly
noun complaisance
Complaisant employees make employers
happy.

477. **compliant** adj. (kəm-pli′ənt)
yielding; complying; submissive
adj. compliable
adv. compliantly
adv. compliably
noun compliableness
noun compliance
noun compliancy
Try to be compliant so you're not known as
defiant.

478. **innominate** adj. (i-nom′ə-nit)
having no name; anonymous
She received a phone message from an innominate caller.

479. **appellation** noun (ap′ə-lā′shən)
a name; a title
He boxes under the appellation of Killer.

480. **appellative** noun (ə-pəl′ə-tiv)
    a name; a title
        adj. appellative—designative; descriptive
        adv. appellatively
        noun appellativeness
            The trucker used the appellative Swamp
            Dog for his CB handle.

481. **cognomen** noun (kog-nō′mən)
    a name; an appellation
        adj. cognominal
            All applications have a space for your cog-
            nomen.

482. **incontrovertible** adj. (in′kon-trə-vûr′tə-bəl)
    indisputable; can't be argued; undeniable
        adv. incontrovertibly
        noun incontrovertibility
        noun incontrovertibleness
            Incontrovertible evidence exists that
            Black Foot Indians once lived in this reg-
            ion.

483. **cogent** adj. (kō′jənt)
    convincing
        adv. cogently
            The debater presented very cogent reasons
            for his view.

166

484. **cogitate** verb (koj′ə-tāt)
   to meditate; to think; to consider
      adj. cogitable—(koj′ə-tə-bəl)
      adj. cogitative—thoughtful
      adv. cogitatively
      noun cogitation—meditation
      noun cogitator—thinker
      noun cogitativeness
         The members were asked to cogitate on the
         proposal before voting.

485. **ingenious** adj. (in-jēn′yəs)
   skillful; clever; inventive
      adv. ingeniously
      noun ingeniousness
      noun ingenuity
         An ingenious carpenter can do wonders
         with used lumber.

486. **ingenuous** adj. (in-jen′yo͞o-əs)
   1. frank; candid
   2. innocent; naive
      adv. ingenuously
      noun ingenuousness
         Ingenuous (innocent) youngsters are una-
         ware of life's harsh realities.

487. **surmise** verb (sûr′mīz)
   to guess; to conjecture
      noun surmise—an educated guess
         I surmise the home team will win.

488. **conjecture** verb (kən-jek′chər)
to guess; to infer
adj. conjecturable
adv. conjecturably
noun conjecturer
noun conjecture—a guess
What do you conjecture the future will hold
for the graduating class?


489. **supposition** noun (sup′ə-zish′ən)
an assumption; that which is supposed
adj. suppositional—supposed or assumed
adj. suppositive
adv. suppostionally
adv. suppositively
The detective's simple supposition helped
solve the crime.


490. **ubiquitous** adj. (yo͞o-bik′wə-təs)
everywhere; omnipresent
adj. ubiquitary
adv. ubiquitously
noun ubiquitousness
noun ubiquity
An ubiquitous ghost haunted the rooms of
the mansion.

491. **anecdote** noun (an′ik-dōt)
    a short story; a narrative
        adj. anecdotal—pertaining to or consisting of
                  anecdotes
        adj. anecdotic
        adj. anecdotical
        noun anecdotage—anecdotes collectively
        noun anecdotist—one who collects or tells
                  anecdotes
        The master of ceremonies told a short introductory anecdote about the guest speaker.


492. **hyperbolic** adj. (hi′pər-bol′ik)
    exaggerated
        adj. hyperbolical
        adv. hyperbolically
        noun hyperbole (hī-pûr′bə-lē)
        noun hyperbolism
        verb hyperbolize (hī-pûr′bə-līz)—to exaggerate
        Science fiction is hyperbolic writing at its ultimate.


493. **peremptory** adj. (pər′əmp-tôr′ē)
    unconditional; absolute; dictatorial; positive in opinion; arrogant
        adv. peremptorily
        noun peremptoriness
        The armed robber made a peremptory demand for all money.

494. **sublime** adj. (sə-blīm′)
supreme; grand; inspiring awe; splendid
adv. sublimely
noun sublimity
noun sublimeness
noun sublime—that which is majestic, supreme, etc.
noun sublimer
verb sublimate—to refine; to purify
Viewing the valley from atop the mountain was a sublime experience.

495. **bevy** noun (bev′ē)
group; collection
The pageant included a bevy of beauties.

496. **ominous** adj. (om′ə-nəs)
threatening
adv. ominously
noun ominousness
Ominous thunder clouds began to appear.

497. **omniscient** adj. (om-nish′ənt)
knowing all things; infinite knowledge
adv. omnisciently
noun omniscience—(om-nish′əns)
Christians worship an omniscient God.

498. **mellifluous** adj. (me-lif′loo-əs)
sweetly or smoothly flowing
adv. mellifluously
noun mellifluousness
A mellifluous speech is enjoyable listening.

499. **melodious** adj. (mə-lō′dē-əs)
   pleasant to hear; tuneful
   adv. melodiously
   noun melodiousness
   A melodious voice is an announcer's asset.

500. **euphonious** adj. (yōō-fō′nē-əs)
   pleasant in sound
   adj. euphonic
   adj. euphonical
   adv. euphoniously
   adv. euphonically
   noun euphoniousness
   noun euphony
   verb euphonize—to make pleasant in sound
   Soft euphonious music is often played in
   supermarkets to relax customers.

1. anachronism  a. study of ancient times
   b. something out of proper time period
   c. wise saying  d. story of a person's life
2. anecdote  a. rule by one person  b. short story
   d. lack of government  d. bishop
3. appellation  a. name  b. original model
   c. passageway  d. stars
4. appellative  a. coziness  b. galaxy  c. title
   d. aquatic
5. auspices  a. guidance  b. exception
   c. frankness  d. loyalty
6. auspicious  a. youthful  b. watery  c. favorable
   d. refined
7. avarice  a. zealous  b. good temper  c. greed
   d. unskilled
8. bevy  a. collection  b. radiance  c. watcher
   d. catastrophe
9. blatant  a. anguish  b. unconcerned
   c. venturesome  d. noisy
10. buffoon  a. clown  b. briefness  c. arrogance
    d. intolerance
11. circuitous  a. booming  b. roundabout
    c. electrical  d. shocking
12. circumlocution  a. endurance  b. round figure
    c. discord  d. indirect expression
13. circumvent  a. avoid  b. kidnap  c. admit
    d. degrade
14. clamorous  a. hard shelled  b. charitable
    c. pleasant  d. noisy
15. cogent  a. highly ornate  b. blessed  c. double
    d. convincing

16. cogitate  a. capture  b. think  c. burp  d. chew
17. cognomen  a. name  b. unknown male
    c. censor  d. hiding place
18. complacent  a. transformed  b. not grateful
    c. rapid  d. pleased
19. complaisant  a. speedy  b. spiritual
    c. comfortable  d. yielding
20. compliant  a. glorious  b. quick  c. mild
    d. submissive
21. compunctious  a. diseased  b. indecisive
    c. plump  d. regretful
22. confection  a. candy  b. small mass
    c. irregularity  d. examination
23. conjecture  a. guess  b. convince  c. think
    d. shorten
24. consternation  a. enclosure  b. fright
    c. diversion  d. crucial point
25. constituent  a. adverse policy  b. expansion
    c. voter  d. friendship
26. covetous  a. greedy  b. fulfilled  c. limited
    d. expensive
27. cupidity  a. communication  b. greed
    c. nakedness  d. love
28. deify  a. worship  b. recover  c. ignore
    d. kneel
29. divergent  a. industrious  b. different
    c. vigorous  d. indirect
30. edacity  a. act of learning
    b. study of urban areas  c. act of gluttony
    d. recovery
31. efflorescent  a. blossoming  b. flammable
    c. leisurely  d. nice

32. erotic  a. strangely different
    b. pertaining to sensual love  c. startling
    d. soft
33. eschew  a. maul  b. merge  c. avoid  d. grind
34. euphonious  a. able to spell well
    b. harsh sounding  c. dishonorable
    d. pleasant in sound
35. evitable  a. civilized  b. avoidable  c. thorough
    d. creative
36. exotic  a. foreign  b. current  c. bloody
    d. showy
37. facetious  a. peculiar  b. humorous
    c. featureless  d. mischievous
38. flapdoodle  a. joke  b. scribble  c. foolish talk
    d. awkwardness
39. flippant  a. gymnastical  b. lithe
    c. able to dance  d. disrespectful
40. fraught  a. manageable  b. filled with
    c. liveable  d. ghostly
41. fruition  a. narrowness  b. completion
    c. splendor  d. vulgar dialogue
42. garrulous  a. protective  b. talkative
    c. enlarging  d. sour
43. glib  a. slippery  b. quick but clumsy
    c. fluent but thoughtless  d. loose in morals
44. gluttony  a. act of talking excessively
    b. context  c. act of eating excessively
    c. scarcity
45. hyperbolic  a. exaggerated  b. scholastic
    c. closely confined  d. high-strung
46. incongruous  a. out-of-place  b. next to
    c. obligatory  d. not stable

47. incontrovertible  a. controversial  b. obese
    c. private  d. indisputable
48. inevitable  a. unavoidable  b. dying
    c. monstrous  d. jolly
49. ingenious  a. causing pain  b. capable
    c. skillful  d. wonderful
50. ingenuous  a. childish  b. clever  c. frank
    d. fun loving
51. innominate  a. anonymous
    b. recommendatory  c. mutual  d. reasonless
52. insatiable  a. extremely unaware
    b. quietly reassuring  c. overbearing
    d. incapable of satisfaction
53. insipid  a. over and above  b. least  c. lumpy
    d. uninteresting
54. jejune  a. drooping  b. like spring  c. dull
    d. joyous
55. jesting  a. prevailing  b. artificial  c. playful
    d. selfish
56. jocose  a. humorous  b. gloomy  c. driven
    d. fully equipped
57. jocular  a. making jokes  b. arched
    c. humorless  d. tolerable
58. jocund  a. hot  b. cheerful  c. withdrawn
    d. petrified
59. levity  a. purposeful  b. lightness  c. curious
    d. weighty
60. loquacious  a. of great power
    b. below surface  c. talkative  d. amusing
61. mellifluous  a. smoothly flowing  b. racial
    c. pleasant to taste  d. respected
62. melodious  a. senile  b. urgent  c. sincere
    d. tuneful

63. meticulous   a. encouraging   b. careful
    c. physically exhausted   d. external
64. ominous   a. everywhere   b. wandering
    c. violent   d. threatening
65. omniscient   a. popular   b. all-knowing
    c. prognostic   d. infirm
66. omnivorous   a. universal power   b. not limited
    c. devouring everything   d. infinite
67. palaver   a. idle talk   b. horse   c. conclusion
    d. important discussion
68. parlance   a. legal   b. wild party   c. language
    d. purchase
69. pedagogue   a. teacher   b. preacher
    c. substitute   d. leeway
70. peremptory   a. critical   b. professorial
    c. dictatorial   d. needless
71. perfunctory   a. flamboyant
    b. done mechanically   c. uncanny
    d. inexperienced
72. permeable   a. allowing passage   b. restricted
    c. wide-open   d. medieval
73. persnickety   a. flowery   b. beholden   c. fussy
    d. miserably poor
74. pervasive   a. calm   b. callous   c. cancelable
    d. penetrating
75. prattle   a. thrust   b. squeal   c. foolish talk
    d. serious discussion
76. proffer   a. stab   b. squeeze   c. decide   d. offer
77. propitious   a. squeezable   b. favorable
    c. dislikable   d. sweetly flowing
78. prosaic   a. uninteresting   b. dismissible
    c. resistant   d. nimble

79. punctilious a. aggressive b. divinely inspired
    c. careful about conduct d. terrific
80. rapacious a. greedy b. ageless c. trifling
    d. finicky
81. remorseful a. effective b. full of deep regret
    c. forgetful d. picturesque
82. replete a. imaginary b. delicate c. filled
    d. too particular
83. ribald a. offensive smell b. massive c. vulgar
    d. sloppy
84. rueful a. well-bred b. prankish c. deplorable
    d. ridiculous
85. satiate a. stir up b. express concern c. glut
    d. rear
86. scrupulous a. suitable b. menacing c. upright
    d. by chance
87. semblance a. slight fault
    b. premonition of evil c. special talent
    d. outward appearance
88. sublime a. supreme b. shady c. shoddy
    d. shaky
89. superficial a. impulsive b. near the surface
    c. much strength d. fruitful
90. supposition a. motion b. essence
    c. assumption c. coalition
91. surfeit a. gather information
    b. fill beyond desire c. cover with thin layer
    d. speak stupidly
92. surmise a. store up b. decorate c. guess
    d. leap playfully
93. tutelage a. successfulness b. guidance
    c. brotherhood d. feasibility

94. twaddle   a. degrading information
    b. sweet substance   c. subversion
    d. foolish talk
95. ubiquitous   a. brief and meaningful   b. wicked
    c. everywhere   d. foreign
96. vapid   a. swift   b. illiterate   c. lusty
    d. no liveliness
97. vociferant   a. itchy   b. noisy   c. antiquated
    d. hapless
98. vociferous   a. irritating   b. out-of-date
    c. unfortunate   d. clamorous
99. voracious   a. snarling   b. greedy   c. noisy
    d. wasted away
100. waggish   a. listless   b. unintelligent
    c. awkward   d. humorous

## Test 5

### Answers

| | | | |
|---|---|---|---|
| 1. b | 26. a | 51. a | 76. d |
| 2. b | 27. b | 52. d | 77. b |
| 3. a | 28. a | 53. d | 78. a |
| 4. c | 29. b | 54. c | 79. c |
| 5. a | 30. c | 55. c | 80. a |
| 6. c | 31. a | 56. a | 81. b |
| 7. c | 32. b | 57. a | 82. c |
| 8. a | 33. c | 58. b | 83. c |
| 9. d | 34. d | 59. b | 84. c |
| 10. a | 35. b | 60. c | 85. c |
| 11. b | 36. a | 61. a | 86. c |
| 12. d | 37. b | 62. d | 87. d |
| 13. a | 38. c | 63. b | 88. a |
| 14. d | 39. d | 64. d | 89. b |
| 15. d | 40. b | 65. b | 90. c |
| 16. b | 41. b | 66. c | 91. b |
| 17. a | 42. b | 67. a | 92. c |
| 18. d | 43. c | 68. c | 93. b |
| 19. d | 44. c | 69. a | 94. d |
| 20. d | 45. a | 70. c | 95. c |
| 21. d | 46. a | 71. b | 96. d |
| 22. a | 47. d | 72. a | 97. b |
| 23. a | 48. a | 73. c | 98. d |
| 24. b | 49. c | 74. d | 99. b |
| 25. c | 50. c | 75. c | 100. d |

## SCORING

Correct answers

    100-90 = A (excellent)

      89-80 = B (good)

      79-70 = C (fair)

      69-60 = D (poor)

      59- 0 = E (Start over!)

Score before word study _____

Score after word study _____

501. **enhance** verb (in-hans′)
   to improve; to intensify; to increase
   noun enhancement
   noun enhancer
      The second job will enhance his financial
      condition.


502. **meliorate** verb (mēl′yə-rāt)
   to improve; ameliorate; to make better
   adj. meliorative
   adj. meliorable
   noun melioration—betterment
   noun meliority—superiority
   noun meliorator
      Unemployment payments meliorate the fi-
      nancial stresses of laid-off workers.


503. **refurbish** verb (re fûr′bish)
   to renovate; to polish up
      To refurbish the old theater would be ex-
      pensive.


504. **embellish** verb (im-bel′ish)
   to beautify; to adorn; to decorate; to garnish
   noun embellishment
      Aluminum siding was used to embellish the
      old house.

505. **paradox** noun (par′ə-doks)
    something absurd, yet truthful; something for
    the most part false or absurd
    adj. paradoxical
    adv. paradoxically
    noun paradoxicality
    noun paradoxicalness
        The comical play was a paradox about the
        life of Caesar.

506. **ironic** adj. (ī-ron′ik)
    meaning the opposite of what is said or portrayed
    adj. ironical
    adv. ironically
    noun ironicalness
    noun irony
        Isn't it ironic that the salesman claims it's
        the best car made but doesn't own one
        himself?

507. **lucrative** adj. (lōō′krə-tiv)
    profitable
    adv. lucratively
    noun lucrativeness
        Many hobbies have developed into lucra-
        tive professions.

508. **gainful** adj. (gān′fəl)
    profitable
    adv. gainfully
    noun gainfulness
        During recessionary periods gainful
        employment opportunities disappear.

509. **remuneration** noun (ri-my$\overline{oo}$′nə-rā′ shən)
  a reward; a pay
    adj. remunerable—profitable
    adj. remunerative
    adv. remuneratively
    noun remunerativeness
    noun remunerability
    noun remunerator
      Remuneration came in the form of a substantial monthly check.

510. **compensation** noun (kom′pən-sā′shən)
  a reward; a payment
    adj. compensative
    adj. compensatory
    adj. compensational
    noun compensator
    verb compensate—to pay
      Cash compensation was given the laborer for his efforts.

511. **recompense** noun (rek′əm-pens)
  a payment; a reward; a compensation
    verb recompense—to reward; to pay
      He received a recompense for services rendered.

512. **repertoire** noun (rep′ər-twär)
  a list of songs, plays, operas or the like that an individual is prepared to perform
      The band chosen for the festivity promised a large repertoire of music.

513. **transcend** verb (tran-send′)
    to rise above; to surpass; to excel; exceed
        adj. transcendent—of very high degree; sur-
                        passing; excelling
        adj. transcendental
        adv. transcendently
        adv. transcendentally
        noun transcendence
        noun transcendency
        noun transcendentness
        The candidate wanted to transcend the
        mudslinging initiated by his opponent.

514. **ratiocination** noun (rash′ē-os′ə-nā′shən)
    a reasoning process; reasoning
        adj. ratiocinative
        noun ratiocinator
        verb ratiocinate—to reason
        The movie required the audience to use
        ratiocination in solving the crime.

515. **indicative** adj. (in-dik′ə-tiv)
    suggestive
        adv. indicatively
        The boy's sloppy table manners are indica-
        tive of poor parental teachings.

516. **frugal** adj. (fr$\overline{oo}$´gəl)
    1. careful in spending; avoiding waste
    2. costing little; meager
    adv. frugally
    noun frugalness
    noun frugality
        The frugal man enjoyed large interest returns from his savings account.

517. **parsimonious** adj. (pär´sə-mō´nē-əs)
    stingy; tightwad
    adv. parsimoniously
    noun parsimony
    noun parsimoniousness
        The parsimonious man wouldn't buy a pan, so warmed his meals in a can.

518. **niggardly** adj. (nig´ərd-lē)
    1. stingy
    2. scanty; insufficient
    adj. niggard—stingy
    adv. niggardly
    noun niggardliness
    noun niggard—a stingy person
        He receives a niggardly wage.

519. **penurious** adj. (pə n$\breve{oo}$r´ē-əs)
    1. stingy
    2. poor
    adv. penuriously
    noun penuriousness
    noun penury—extreme poverty
        The penurious man will not give to charity.

520. **indigent** adj. (in′də-jənt)
poor
adv. indigently
noun indigence
noun indigency
He said he was so indigent that he broke his mirrors so he wouldn't have to watch himself starve to death.

521. **necessitous** adj. (nə-ses′ə-təs)
1. poor; needy
2. urgent
adv. necessitiously
noun necessitousness
Welfare programs help necessitous families.

522. **destitute** adj. (des′tə-to͞ot)
extremely poor; needy
noun destituteness
noun destitution
The father's long illness left the family destitute.

523. **indigenous** adj. (in-dij′ə-nəs)
native to
adj. indigenal
adv. indigenously
noun indigenousness
noun indigenity
noun indigene (in′də-jēn)—a person or thing that is native
Orange trees are indigenous to warm climates.

524. **innate** adj. (in′āt)
   inborn
      adv. innately
      noun innateness
         His mother-in-law has the innate characteristic of talking too much.

525. **indignant** adj. (in-dig′nənt)
   angry for good reasons
      adv. indignantly
      noun indignation
         The homeowner was indignant over the higher assessed valuation of his house.

526. **indignity** noun (in-dig′nə-tē)
   an insult; an injury to one's dignity
         Please don't subject her to such an indignity.

527. **complicity** noun (kəm-plis′ə-tē)
   1. a participation; an involvement
   2. complexity
         Keeping your complicity in this scandal a secret is impossible.

528. **labyrinth** noun (lab′ə-rinth)

    a maze of winding and intricate paths or passages

      adj. labyrinthine (lab′ə-rin′thin)—pertaining to a labyrinth; intricate; confusing

      adj. labyrinthian

      adj. labyrinthic

      adj. labyrinthical

      adv. labyrinthically

      The story was about two boys lost in a labyrinth of secret caves.

529. **perjury** noun (pûr′jə-rē)

    the act of not telling the truth under oath

      adj. perjured—guilty of perjury

      adv. perjuredly

      noun perjurer—one who makes false statements

      verb perjure—to make a false statement

      Because he gave false testimony, a charge of perjury was instituted.

530. **prevaricate** verb (pri-var′ə-kāt)

    to lie; to speak in a deceptive manner

      noun prevaricator

      noun prevarication

      An old adage (saying) implies your nose will grow longer if you prevaricate.

531. **equivocal** adj. (i-kwiv′ə-kəl)
     dubious; questionable; ambiguous; suspicious
     adj. equivocatory
     adv. equivocally
     noun equivocation
     noun equivocalness
     noun equivocator
     verb equivocate (i-kwiv′ə-kāt)—to use am-
                       biguous language to mis-
                       lead or deceive
     The lawyer's alleged equivocal dealings
     were being reviewed by the board.


532. **nebulous** adj. (neb′yə-ləs)
     hazy; vague
     adv. nebulously
     noun nebulousness
     noun nebulosity
     The answer was discreetly nebulous.


533. **promulgate** verb (prom′əl-gāt)
     to publish; to announce; to proclaim formally
     noun promulgation
     noun promulgator
     verb promulge (prō-mulj′)
     Tomorrow the committee will promulgate
     the actual vote on banning throw-away
     bottles.


189

534. **sagacious** adj. (sə-gā′shəs)
    wise; keen in judgment
      adv. sagaciously
      noun sagaciousness
      noun sagacity (sə-gas′ə-tē)—wisdom and shrewdness
      His sagacious assessment of the economy contributed to his successful stock market venture.

535. **astute** adj. (ə-sto͞ot′)
    wise; keen in judgment; sagacious
      adj. astucious
      adj. astutious
      adv. astutely
      noun astuteness
      A good command of vocabulary makes one sound impressively astute.

536. **prudent** adj. (pro͞od′nt)
    wise; keen in judgment; judicious
      adv. prudently
      noun prudence
      She made a prudent decision to stock up on coffee before poor growing weather sent coffee prices skyrocketing.

537. **judicious** adj. (jo͞o-dish′əs)
    wise; keen in judgment; prudent
      adv. judiciously
      noun judiciousness
      It would be judicious to postpone the trip until it stops snowing.

538. **perspicacious** adj. (pûr′spə-kā′shəs)
   wise; keen in judgment or understanding; having insight
      adv. perspicaciously
      noun perspicaciousness
      noun perspecacity
         The perspicacious investigator was in great demand by insurance companies.

539. **acumen** noun (ak′yōō-mən)
   keenness of mind
         Because of his proven business acumen, he is often asked to comment on the commodity futures.

540. **discerning** adj. (di-sûr′ning)
   quick to see; quick to recognize; quick to distinguish
      adv. discerningly
      noun discerner
      noun discernment
      verb discern—to recognize; to distinguish
         The discerning jury found many inconsistencies in the testimony.

541. **discreet** adj. (dis-krēt′)
   1. wise; cautious
   2. tactful especially in dealing with people
      adv. discreetly
      noun discreetness
         A discreet effort was made not to mention the player's former prison record.

542. **tact** noun (takt)
  1. a keen sense of what to say or do
  2. a skill in dealing with people or difficult situations
    adj. tactful
    adv. tactfully
    noun tactfulness
      The arbitrator exhibited a great deal of tact in bringing the two sides together.


543. **erudite** adj. (er´yŏŏ-dit)
    learned; scholarly
    adv. eruditely
    noun eruditeness
    noun erudition
      It was an erudite theory but would never work in reality.


544. **circumspect** adj. (sûr´kəm-spekt)
    careful; attentive; watchful; cautious; prudent
    adj. circumspective
    adv. circumspectly
    noun circumspectness
    noun circumspection
      Circumspect behavior is a must for the lion trainer.


545. **prodigy** noun (prod´ə-jē)
    a person born with extraordinary gifts or powers; a genius
      The child was a musical prodigy.

546. **precocious** adj. (pri-kō′shəs)
  unusually advanced for one's age
    adv. precociously
    noun precociousness
    noun precocity (pri-kos′ə-tē)
      The precocious child pianist was playing
      Mozart at age seven.

547. **provident** adj. (prov′ə-dənt)
  making plans for the future; exercising foresight
    adv. providently
      The provident buggy whip manufacturer
      cancelled expansion plans with the advent
      (arrival) of the automobile.

548. **ken** noun (ken)
  knowledge; comprehension
      Thermokinematics is beyond most
      people's ken.

549. **portend** verb (pôr-tend′)
  to predict; to warn; to forecast
      The ominous (threatening) clouds portend
      a thunderstorm.

550. **presage** verb (pri-sāj)
  to foretell; to forecast; to predict; to warn of
    noun presage (pres′ij)—an omen
    noun presager
      Broken mirrors presage years of bad luck.

551. **prognosticate** verb (prog-nos′tə-kāt)
    to predict; to foretell future happenings
        adj. prognosticative—predicting; indicating
        adj. prognostic
        noun prognostication—the act of prognos-
                        ticating; a prediction
        noun prognosticator—one who forecasts or
                        predicts
        noun prognostic—a prediction; a forecast
        noun prognosis—a prediction; a forecast
        The weatherman was respected for his abil-
        ity to prognosticate the weather accu-
        rately.

552. **prophesy** verb (prof′ə-sī)
    to predict; to foretell
        noun prophecy (prof′ə-sē)—a prediction
        noun prophesier
        Avoid quacks who profess (declare)
        the ability to prophesy future events.

553. **forebode** verb (fôr-bōd′)
    1. to predict (usually something harmful or evil)
    2. to feel something evil about to happen
        adj. foreboding—predicting (especially evil)
        adv. forebodingly
        noun foreboder
        noun foreboding—a prediction; a feeling that
                        something evil is about to
                        happen
        The harsh tremors no doubt forebode an
        earthquake.

554. **portent** noun (pôr′tent)
    a sign; a forewarning; a prediction
      adj. portentous—threatening; predicting
      adv. portentously
      noun portentousness
        The superstitious man regarded the black
        cat as a portent of evil.

555. **clairvoyant** adj. (klâr-voi′ənt)
    having power to see beyond normal range; hav-
    ing insight
      noun clairvoyance
      noun clairvoyant—one who has insight
        A clairvoyant stock trader would be a very
        rich one.

556. **prescient** adj. (prē′shē-ənt)
    having knowledge of events before they take
    place; having foreknowledge; having foresight
      adv. presciently
      noun prescience
        If the divorcée had prescient powers, it's
        doubtful that she would be in her present
        state.

557. **abstruse** adj. (ab-stroos′)
    hard to understand; hidden
      adv. abstrusely
      noun abstruseness
        Students often need the instructor's help in
        reading the abstruse works of great au-
        thors.

558. **profound** adj. (prə-found′)
   1. intense
   2. hard to understand
   3. deep
   4. intellectually deep
   adv. profoundly
   noun profoundness
   noun profundity
   > His thoughts on Sartre's work were
   > original and profound.

559. **precept** noun (prē′sept)
   a rule of conduct
   adj. preceptive
   adv. preceptively
   > "Do unto others as you would have them
   > do unto you," is a precept we should all
   > heed.

560. **adage** noun (ad′ij)
   a wise saying
   > An adage well worth memorizing is "He
   > who thinks he is on top of the world should
   > keep in mind that the world turns over
   > every twenty-four hours."

561. **aphorism** noun (af'ə-riz'əm)
    a wise saying
        adj. aphoristic
        adj. aphoristical
        adj. aphorismic
        adj. aphorismatic
        adv. aphoristically
        noun aphorist—a person who invents or uses
                    aphorisms
        verb aphorize—to invent or use aphorisms
          An aphorism often helps in stressing a
          point.


562. **proverb** noun (prov'ərb)
    a wise saying
        Grandfather had a proverb for every occa-
        sion.


563. **maxim** noun (mak'sim)
    a wise saying
        The maxim "A little extra effort is the dif-
        ference between good and great," ought
        never be forgotten.


564. **sententious** adj. (sen-ten'shəs)
    abounding with short wise sayings; aphoristic
        adv. sententiously
        noun sententiousness
        noun sententiousity
        The Bible is written in a sententious style.

565. **tacit** adj. (tas′it)

    silent; unspoken; not put into words; understood

    adv. tacitly

    noun tacitness

        Let us bow our heads in tacit prayer.


566. **taciturn** adj. (tas′ə-tûrn)

    not inclined to talk very much

    adv. taciturnly

    noun taciturnity

        People called him arrogant, but he was really just a taciturn person.


567. **reticent** adj. (ret′ə-sənt)

    not inclined to talk much; quiet in manner; taciturn

    adv. reticently

    noun reticency

    noun reticence

        A reticent person says less, but hears more.


568. **diffident** adj. (dif′ə-dənt)

    shy

    adv. diffidently

    noun diffidence

        The kid was diffident in public, but a little hellion at home.

569. **coy** adj. (koi)

  shy; feigning shyness to get attention
  adj. coyish
  adv. coyly
  noun coyness

   She pretended to be coy to get a date with
   Roy.

570. **timorous** adj. (tim′ər-əs)

  1. fearful; afraid
  2. timid
  adv. timorously
  noun timorousness

   The broker told the timorous investor the
   market had reached bottom and would now
   rocket upward.

571. **coquette** noun (kō-ket′)

  a flirt; a woman who tries to attract men's affec-
  tions
  adj. coquettish
  adv. coquettishly
  noun coquettishness

   Loving her as he did, Jack wanted to believe
   that she was not a coquette, but his alone.

572. **empathy** noun (em′pə-thē)
the perception or understanding of another's
feelings or spirit; a feeling for another
adj. empathic
adv. empathically
verb empathize
We all have empathy for the family that
loses everything in a house fire.

573. **vicarious** adj. (vī-kâr′ē-əs)
done, performed, received, or suffered in place
of another; acting for another; substituted
adv. vicariously
noun vicariousness
Grandma felt vicarious thrills watching her
grandchildren Christmas morning.

574. **subrogate** verb (sub′rō-gāt)
to substitute
noun subrogation
Perhaps we should subrogate the sugar
with an artificial sweetener.

575. **supersede** verb (soo′pər-sēd′)
1. to replace (to replace usually with something
superior, newer or more effective)
2. to cause to be set aside
noun superseder
noun supersedure
noun supersession
Some people actually thought the au-
tomobile would never supersede the horse.

576. **supplant** verb (sə-plant′)
   1. to replace
   2. to take place of another by trickery
   3. to uproot; to overthrow
   noun supplantation
   noun supplanter
      For a new leader to supplant the present
      militarily strong dictator would be impos-
      sible.

577. **temporize** verb (tem′pə-rīz)
   to act evasively to gain time; to stall
   adv. temporizingly
   noun temporization
   noun temporizer
      Temporize no longer; we must have a deci-
      sion immediately!

578. **precarious** adj. (pri-kâr′ē-əs)
   dangerous; uncertain; hazardous
   adv. precariously
   noun precariousness
      The mountain goat stood on a precarious
      ledge overlooking the valley.

579. **perilous** adj. (per′əl-əs)
   dangerous
   adv. perilously
   noun peril
   noun perilousness
      A perilous road twisted its way up the steep
      mountain.

580. **construe** verb (kən-strōō′)
    to explain; to translate; to interpret
      adj. construable
      noun construer
      noun construability
        It is very difficult to construe from such befuddling (confusing) statements your true ideas on the subject.

581. **purport** verb (pûr′port)
    to profess; to express; to imply; to claim
      adv. purportedly
      noun purport—meaning; significance
        Neighbors purport he's so stupid that he once watered his garden with vodka so it would produce stewed tomatoes.

582. **profess** verb (prə-fes′)
    to declare; to assert
      adv. professedly
      noun profession—a declaration
        All his customers will profess their satisfaction with the product.

583. **consummate** verb (kon′sə-māt)
    to complete; to finish
      adj. consummate (kən-sum′it)—perfect; complete
      adj. consummative
      adv. consummately
      noun consummator
      noun consummation—fulfillment
        Let's consummate the bargain with a handshake.

584. **retrogress** verb (ret′rə-gres)
to go backward into an earlier condition, usually worse
adj. retrogressive
adv. retrogressively
noun retrogression
Inflation caused the stock market to retrogress to low levels.

585. **retrospective** adj. (ret′rə-spek′tiv)
looking backward; retroactive
adv. retrospectively
noun retrospection
noun retrospect—a backward look
verb retrospect—to look back upon
The commission took a retrospective look at the initial goals of the program.

586. **tenuous** adj. (ten′yŏŏ-əs)
slim; flimsy; unsubstantial
adv. tenuously
noun tenuousness
noun tenuity
Teachers hear tenuous excuses daily.

587. **tenable** adj. (ten′ə-bəl)
capable of being maintained or defended
adv. tenably
noun tenability
noun tenableness
All commissioners agreed the new zoning ordinance was tenable.

588. **tenacious** adj. (ti-nā′shəs)
  1. stubborn; holding fast
  2. retentive—as a tenacious memory
    adv. tenaciously
    noun tenaciousness
    noun tenacity
      The tenacious landowner would not grant
      an easement to the gas company.

589. **pertinacious** adj. (pûr′tə-nā′shəs)
    holding tenaciously to a purpose or opinion;
    stubborn; persistent
      adv. pertinaciously
      noun pertinaciousness
      noun pertinacity
        Others gave up, but the pertinacious pros-
        pector continued to pan for gold.

590. **usurp** verb (yōō-sûrp′)
    to seize and hold an office, right, or power of
    another; to take arrogantly
      adv. usurpingly
      noun usurper
      noun usurpation
        The goal of the rebel lieutenant was to
        usurp the authority of his commander.

591. **pandemonium** noun (pan′də-mō′nē-əm)
    a wild uproar; confusion
      Pandemonium broke loose when the cat
      walked by the dog kennel.

592. **brouhaha** noun (broo′hä-hä)
    an uproar
        A brouhaha developed over the referee's decision.


593. **pursuant** adv. (pər-soo′ənt)
    according; conformably (usually followed by to)
        adj. pursuant—done in accordance with; pursuing
    adv. pursuantly
    noun pursuance—the act of pursuing (usually followed by of)
        The payment was made pursuant to the terms in the land contract.


594. **diminution** noun (dim′ə-noo′shən)
    the act of diminishing or lessening; a reduction; a decrease
        A gradual diminution of our natural resources is occurring.


595. **diminutive** adj. (di-min′yə-tiv)
    1. small
    2. diminishing
        adv. diminutively
        noun diminutive—anything small
        noun diminutiveness
        Due to a lack of rain his garden produced all diminutive fruits and vegetables.

596. **apprise** verb (ə-prīz′)
　　　 to notify; to inform
　　　　 noun appriser
　　　　 noun apprisement
　　　　　 Police apprise arrested persons of their
　　　　　 rights.

597. **apprize** verb (ə-prīz′)
　　　 to appraise
　　　　　 The bank will apprize the deceased man's
　　　　　 estate.

598. **efficacious** adj. (ef′ə-kā′shəs)
　　　 effective; producing a desired result
　　　　 adv. efficaciously
　　　　 noun efficaciousness
　　　　 noun efficacy—effectiveness
　　　　　 The patient received efficacious medicine
　　　　　 for his illness.

599. **chafe** verb (chāf)
　　　 1. to irritate; to annoy
　　　 2. to make sore rubbing
　　　　 noun chafe—an irritation
　　　　　 Don't chafe the bull unless you can outrun
　　　　　 him.

600. **chaff** verb (chaf)
　　　 to poke fun; to tease
　　　　 noun chaff—good natured kidding
　　　　　 Chaff him with ethnic jokes and he'll surely
　　　　　 become angered.

## Test 6

1. abstruse  a. foolhardy  b. unwise
   c. hard to understand  d. easily perceived
2. acumen  a. group of businessmen  b. company
   c. slow  d. keenness of mind
3. adage  a. clever maneuver  b. old times  c. gist
   d. wise saying
4. aphorism  a. manipulation  b. skillfulness
   c. theme  d. wise saying
5. apprise  a. award  b. take back  c. notify
   d. harass
6. apprize  a. arrest  b. obstruct  c. appraise
   d. insult
7. astute  a. disregarding  b. wise  c. well-fed
   d. relevant
8. brouhaha  a. uproar  b. settlement  c. laughter
   d. humorist
9. chafe  a. annoy  b. drink  c. calm down
   d. run away from
10. chaff  a. fritter  b. tease  c. fondle  d. compute
11. circumspect  a. grueling  b. rough mannered
    c. cautious and wise  d. indirect
12. clairvoyant  a. theatrical  b. shouting
    c. snobbish  d. having insight
13. compensation  a. threat  b. suffering
    c. laboriousness  d. payment
14. complicity  a. urbaneness  b. uprightness
    c. participation  d. failure
15. construe  a. collect  b. raise crops  c. swindle
    d. interpret
16. consummate  a. flock to  b. tighten up
    c. complete  d. overstock
17. coquette  a. game  b. glutton  c. flirt  d. pygmy

18. coy  a. domineering  b. inappropriate  c. bold
    d. shy
19. destitute  a. poor  b. untidy  c. civilized
    d. grisly
20. diffident  a. varied  b. shy  c. unusual
    d. insolent
21. diminution  a. weakness from age
    b. reduction  c. surprising increase  d. guilt
22. diminutive  a. worn-out  b. small  c. enlarging
    d. wrongful
23. discerning  a. quick to see
    b. quick to criticize  c. headless  d. blessed
24. discreet  a. scanty  b. wise  c. flashy
    d. dependable
25. efficacious  a. effective  b. effortless  c. vast
    d. haphazard
26. embellish  a. make rich  b. chew  c. rehearse
    d. adorn
27. empathy  a. regretfulness  b. immigration
    c. feeling for another  d. ungratefulness
28. enhance  a. improve  b. incarcerate
    c. compose  d. make whole
29. equivocal  a. straightforward  b. welcomed
    c. not transferable  d. dubious
30. erudite  a. scholarly  b. speechless
    c. senseless  d. disturbed
31. forebode  a. impair  b. cancel  c. sanctify
    d. predict
32. frugal  a. lacking room
    b. entirely without merit  c. naive
    d. careful in spending
33. gainful  a. profitable  b. hard to find
    c. highly regarded  d. incorrigible

34. indicative  a. needy  b. suggestive
    c. very lenient  d. tough
35. indigenous  a. warm  b. inflated  c. immaterial
    d. native to
36. indigent  a. poor  b. relentless  c. well-off
    d. incompetent
37. indignant  a. destitute  b. extreme
    c. hampering  d. angry for good reasons
38. indignity  a. insult  b. sudden invasion
    c. violation  d. poverty
39. innate  a. inborn  b. silly  c. subsequent
    d. tricky
40. ironic  a. meaning the opposite  b. similar
    c. having ability to see ahead  d. flattened
41. judicious  a. unchaste  b. wise  c. harmful
    d. intent
42. ken  a. secret  b. knowledge
    c. harmoniousness  d. comedy
43. labyrinth  a. interim  b. burial vault  c. maze
    d. field of crops
44. lucrative  a. loosely united  b. radiant
    c. profitable  d. tasteless
45. maxim  a. delicious drink  b. inverse ratio
    c. wise saying  d. untrue story
46. meliorate  a. abuse  b. underrate
    c. move slowly  d. improve
47. nebulous  a. apt to be deleted  b. fatigued
    c. incapable of injury  d. hazy
48. necessitous  a. poor  b. able  c. not willing
    d. narrow-minded
49. niggardly  a. derogatory  b. stingy  c. slangy
    d. sleek

50. pandemonium  a. peacefulness
    b. slapstick humor  c. wild uproar
    d. aimlessness
51. paradox  a. sleepiness  b. two dots  c. insanity
    d. something absurd yet truthful
52. parsimonious  a. inconceivable  b. stimulating
    c. not frank  d. stingy
53. penurious  a. provoking  b. not noticeable
    c. stingy  d. open
54. perilous  a. dangerous  b. stingy
    c. hidden in meaning  d. beady
55. perjury  a. curse  b. act of not telling truth
    c. act of stealing  d. person sitting in judgment
56. perspicacious  a. keen in judgment  b. lethal
    c. gruesome  d. spacious
57. pertinacious  a. derelict  b. stubborn
    c. mocking  d. impure in thought
58. portend  a. intervene  b. carry  c. predict
    d. free
59. portent  a. token  b. statement of policy
    ill luck  d. forewarning
60. precarious  a. alive and well  b. faulty
    c. dangerous  d. frightening
61. precept  a. introduction  b. index
    c. little spirit  d. rule of conduct
62. precocious  a. dangerous
    b. having a positive attitude  c. gentle
    d. advanced for one's age
63. presage  a. defraud  b. appease  c. forecast
    d. cause to become sick
64. prescient  a. preceding  b. having foresight
    c. strictly accurate  d. prehistoric
65. prevaricate  a. lie  b. warn  c. deny  d. vex

66. prodigy  a. gifted person
    b. retarded individual  c. nonexistence
    d. unsophistication
67. profess  a. pledge  b. declare  c. speed up
    d. swear
68. profound  a. fascinating  b. disguised
    c. intellectually deep  d. hard to please
69. prognosticate  a. identify  b. advocate
    c. tone down  d. predict
70. promulgate  a. announce  b. give birth
    c. proofread  d. contribute to progress
71. prophesy  a. predict  b. promise  c. dabble
    d. talk intellectually
72. proverb  a. middle ground  b. denial
    c. main point  d. wise saying
73. provident  a. sentimental  b. controllable
    c. visible  d. having foresight
74. prudent  a. steadfast  b. necessary  c. wise
    d. planning ahead
75. purport  a. destroy partially  b. scold
    c. profess  d. push into limelight
76. pursuant  a. democratic  b. according
    c. deserving reward  d. wanted
77. ratiocination  a. reasoning process
    b. proportion  c. rash behavior  d. petty fault
78. recompense  a. reorganization
    b. formal praise  c. comprehensiveness
    d. payment
79. refurbish  a. renovate  b. start over
    c. ease pain  d. repudiate
80. remuneration  a. respectfulness  b. severe
    disapproval  c. retaliation  d. pay

81. repertoire  a. brief remainder  b. vengeance
    c. blame  d. list of songs
82. reticent  a. hard pressed  b. entertaining
    c. articulate  d. quiet in manner
83. retrogress  a. deliver  b. discontinue
    c. go backwards  d. revive
84. retrospective  a. looking backwards
    b. no longer made  c. enlivened  d. stopped
85. sagacious  a. having storybook style
    b. imaginative  c. dilapidated  d. wise
86. sententious  a. long and wordy
    b. extremely short  c. vicious
    d. abounding with wise sayings
87. subrogate  a. substitute
    b. go below water level  c. define  d. trade
88. supersede  a. accelerate  b. turn sharply
    c. replace  d. go after
89. supplant  a. place in ground  b. deposit
    c. take place of another
    d. fight for legal rights
90. tacit  a. suave  b. silent  c. witty
    d. loud and violent
91. taciturn  a. smooth talking
    b. inclined not to talk  c. deserving blame
    d. winding
92. tact  a. small nail
    b. skill in dealing with people
    c. shallow thinker  d. slogan
93. temporize  a. yell and swear  b. stall  c. retire
    d. boil with anger
94. tenable  a. retentive
    b. capable of being defended  c. slim
    d. rash judging of others

95. tenacious  a. defensible  b. unsubstantial
    c. quick to decide  d. stubborn
96. tenuous  a. timid  b. grasping
    c. capable of being maintained  d. flimsy
97. timorous  a. time consuming  b. sickly looking
    c. foolish  d. fearful of danger
98. transcend  a. go between  b. satisfy fully
    c. rise above  d. live elegantly
99. usurp  a. take arrogantly  b. substitute
    c. overfeed  d. go over and above
100. vicarious  a. pertaining to priesthood
    b. obvious  c. substituted  d. showy

## Test 6

### Answers

| | | | |
|---|---|---|---|
| 1. c | 26. d | 51. d | 76. b |
| 2. d | 27. c | 52. d | 77. a |
| 3. d | 28. a | 53. c | 78. d |
| 4. d | 29. d | 54. a | 79. a |
| 5. c | 30. a | 55. b | 80. d |
| 6. c | 31. d | 56. a | 81. d |
| 7. b | 32. d | 57. b | 82. d |
| 8. a | 33. a | 58. c | 83. c |
| 9. a | 34. b | 59. d | 84. a |
| 10. b | 35. d | 60. c | 85. d |
| 11. c | 36. a | 61. d | 86. d |
| 12. d | 37. d | 62. d | 87. a |
| 13. d | 38. a | 63. c | 88. c |
| 14. c | 39. a | 64. b | 89. c |
| 15. d | 40. a | 65. a | 90. b |
| 16. c | 41. b | 66. a | 91. b |
| 17. c | 42. b | 67. b | 92. b |
| 18. d | 43. c | 68. c | 93. b |
| 19. a | 44. c | 69. d | 94. b |
| 20. b | 45. c | 70. a | 95. d |
| 21. b | 46. d | 71. a | 96. d |
| 22. b | 47. d | 72. d | 97. d |
| 23. a | 48. a | 73. d | 98. c |
| 24. b | 49. b | 74. c | 99. a |
| 25. a | 50. c | 75. c | 100. c |

## SCORING

Correct answers
- 100-90=A (excellent)
- 89-80=B (good)
- 79-70=C (fair)
- 69-60=D (poor)
- 59-  0=E (Start over!)

Score before word study _____

Score after word study _____

601. **incessant** adj. (in-ses′ənt)
continuous; never ceasing
adv. incessantly
noun incessancy
noun incessantness
The incessant talker returned from the beach with a sunburned tongue.

602. **prototype** noun (prō′tə-tīp)
an original model copied by subsequent models
adj. prototypical
adj. prototypic
adj. prototypal
A prototype of the new toy was stolen by the competition.

603. **paragon** noun (par′ə-gon)
a model of excellence
Many agricultural leaders visit his place because it is a paragon of farms.

604. **dogmatic** adj. (dôg-mat′ik)
characterized by authoritative or arrogant assertion of opinions or beliefs; positive; overbearing
adj. dogmatical
adv. dogmatically
noun dogmatism
noun dogmatist
noun dogma—a strongly held belief or principle
noun dogmatics
verb dogmatize
The dogmatic leader was feared by the people.

216

605. **pragmatic** adj. (prag-mat′ik)
1. practical; concerned with practical consequences or values; pertaining to the study of events with stress on cause and effects
2. meddling; officious
3. relating to everyday affairs or business; commonplace
adj. pragmatical
adv. pragmatically
noun pragmaticalness
noun pragmatism
noun pragmatist
noun pragmatic
   The problem was solved in a pragmatic fashion.

606. **mundane** adj. (mun′dān)
ordinary; earthly; routine
adv. mundanely
noun mundaneness
   Eating and sleeping are mundane tasks we all have in common.

607. **gainly** adj. (gān′lē)
graceful
noun gainliness
   A gainly three-year-old filly won the derby.

608. **comely** adj. (kum′lē)
attractive; proper; seemly; graceful
adv. comelily
noun comeliness
   The comely lass was the object of many stares.

609. **aplomb** noun (ə-plom′)
poise; self-confidence
She rides with the aplomb of an experienced equestrian (horserider).

610. **pulchritude** noun (pul′krə-to͞od)
beauty; comeliness; appeal
adj. pulchritudinous—beautiful; lovely
A camper, lacking gratitude, strewed garbage with great magnitude, and destroyed the park's pulchritude.

611. **posit** verb (poz′it)
to place; to put in position
Please posit yourself in the chair and wait.

612. **repository** noun (ri-poz′ə-tôr′ē)
a depository; a place where things are put or deposited
Our front yard seems to be a repository for empty beer cans.

613. **lissome** adj. (lis′əm)
1. supple; agile; limber; bending easily
2. graceful
adv. lissomely
noun lissomeness
The lissome blonde model has posed for some dubious magazines.

614. **lithe** adj. (līth)
> supple; agile; limber; bending easily
>> adv. lithely
>> noun litheness
>>> The more lithe the gymnast, the more successful the gymnast.

615. **pliant** adj. (pli′ənt)
> 1. supple; agile; limber; bending easily
> 2. yielding to persuasion; compliant
>> adv. pliantly
>> noun pliancy
>> noun pliantness
>>> A pliant rubber hose carried water to the livestock across the road.

616. **apocryphal** adj. (ə-pok′rə-fəl)
> false; spurious; of doubtful authorship
>> adv. apocryphally
>> noun apocryphalness
>>> Her apocryphal sorrow fooled no one.

617. **spurious** adj. (spyo͞or′ē-əs)
> false; counterfeit; not genuine
>> adv. spuriously
>> noun spuriousness
>>> Printing spurious money is a federal offense.

219

618. **rectify** verb (rek′tə-fī)
> to correct
>> adj. rectifiable
>> noun rectification
>>> The students were instructed to rectify their mistakes and turn the papers in the next day.

619. **rectitude** noun (rek′tə-tōōd)
> 1. correctness (as in judgment)
> 2. uprightness in conduct; honesty
>> The administrator is known for his rectitude of judgment.

620. **virtuoso** noun (vûr′chōō-ō′sō)
> a person skilled in any area of endeavor; expert
> He was a virtuoso with the violin.

621. **impugn** verb (im-pyōōn′)
> to challenge the validity of; to attack statements or motives
>> adj. impugnable
>> noun impugnation
>> noun impugnment
>> noun impugner
>>> The lawyer attempted to impugn the credibility of the witness.

622. **plausible** adj. (plô′zə-bəl)
    believable; worthy of approval
        adv. plausibly
        noun plausibility
        noun plausibleness
            It seemed like a plausible story, but father
            insisted on more proof.


623. **moribund** adj. (môr′ə-bund)
    dying; on the verge of termination or extinction
        adv. moribundly
        noun moribundity
            The big city is in a moribund condition.


624. **viable** adj. (vī′ə-bəl)
    1. capable of living normally
    2. practicable; workable
        noun viability
            Doctors agree that the human fetus is via-
            ble at about five months.


625. **inept** adj. (in-ept′)
    1. unsuitable
    2. incompetent; awkward
        adv. ineptly
        noun ineptness
        noun ineptitude
            Inept management caused the restaurant to
            go bankrupt.

626. **decimate** verb (des′ə-māt)
to destroy or kill in large numbers
noun decimation
noun decimator
The troops were ordered not to decimate the village.

627. **reciprocal** adj. (ri-sip′rə-kəl)
mutual
adj. reciprocatory
adj. reciprocative
adv. reciprocally
noun reciprocality
noun reciprocal—that which is reciprocal
noun reciprocalness
noun reciprocator
noun reciprocation
noun reciprocity (res′ə-pros′ə-tē)—a mutual exchange
verb reciprocate—to give in return; to exchange mutually
A good discussion involves the reciprocal exchange of ideas.

628. **pusillanimous** adj. (pyōō′sə-lan′ə-məs)
cowardly
adv. pusillanimously
noun pusillanimousness
noun pusillanimity
Critics accused the draft dodgers of being pusillanimous.

629. **puissant** adj. (py$\overline{oo}'$ə-sənt)
powerful; mighty
adv. puissantly
noun puissance—power
The puissant general led the parade.

630. **peccadillo** noun (pek'ə-dil'ō)
A petty fault; a petty offense; a slight sin
Nail biting is considered an annoying peccadillo.

631. **foible** noun (foi'bəl)
a personal weakness; a flaw in character
Her incessant (uninterrupted) talking is by far her most obnoxious foible.

632. **idiosyncrasy** noun (id'ē-ō-sing'krə-sē)
a characteristic; a habit; a personal oddity; a mannerism
adj. idiosyncratic
adv. idiosyncratically
His idiosyncrasy of not tipping infuriates waitresses.

633. **peccable** adj. (pek'ə-bəl)
capable of sinning
noun peccabiality
Mankind is peccable.

634. **supercilious** adj. (so͞o′pər-sil′ē-əs)
  haughty; arrogant; snobbish
    adv. superciliously
    noun superciliousness
      Even their butler has supercilious airs
      (manners).

635. **haughty** adj. (hô′tē)
  supercilious; arrogant; disdainfully proud'
    adv. haughtily
    noun haughtiness
      The haughty millionaire's nose pointed
      skyward as he walked down the street.

636. **multifarious** adj. (mul′tə-fâr′ē-əs)
  diversified; varied; numerous
    adv. multifariously
    noun multifariousness
      She is active in multifarious organizations.

637. **myriad** adj. (mir′ē-əd)
  many; innumerable
    noun myriad—a vast number
      Myriad sightings of UFOs were made last
      year.

638. **tranquil** adj. (trang′kwil)
  quiet; calm
    adv. tranquilly
    noun tranquilness
    noun tranquillity
    noun tranquilization
    noun tranquillizer
    verb tranquilize
      We spent the summer at a lovely and tranquil country cottage.


639. **placate** verb (plā′kāt)
  to appease; to pacify; to calm
    adj. placative
    adj. placatory
    noun placation
    noun placater
      The manager tried to placate the angry customer.


640. **mitigate** verb (mit′ə-gāt)
  to soften; to make less severe
    adj. mitigative
    adj. mitigable
    adj. mitigatory
    noun mitigation
    noun mitigator
      Aspirins mitigate headache pains.

641. **mollify** verb (mol′ə-fī)
    to soften; to make less severe; to soothe anger
      adj. mollifiable
      adv. mollifyingly
      noun mollification
      noun mollifier
        The mother used every suggestion in the child-rearing book to mollify her hysterical child.

642. **allay** verb (ə-lā′)
    to quiet; to appease; to mitigate
      noun allayer
        Allay your fears!

643. **alleviate** verb (ə-lē′vē-āt)
    to lessen; to make lighter; to mitigate
      adj. alleviative
      adj. alleviatory
      noun alleviation
      noun alleviative—something that alleviates
      noun alleviator
        To alleviate punishment would be to encourage crime.

644. **extenuating** adj. (ik-sten′yōō-ā′ting)
tending to lessen guilt or horribleness of a crime;
tending to make less serious
adj. extenuative
adj. extenuatory
adv. extenuatingly
noun extenuator
noun extenuation
verb extenuate—to lessen the seriousness of
a fault, crime, etc.
The defendant's attorney listed the extenuating circumstances.


645. **mince** verb (mins)
to soften; to tone down
noun mincer
The mayor didn't mince words with his critics.


646. **platonic** adj. (plə-ton′ik)
devoid of sensual feeling or desire
adv. platonically
She proposed that they have only a platonic relationship.


647. **potable** adj. (pō′tə-bəl)
drinkable; suitable for drinking
noun potable—a drink
Water from the polluted creek is not potable.

648. **ineffable** adj. (in-ef′ə-bəl)
    inexpressible; too overpowering for words
      adv. ineffably
      noun ineffability
      noun ineffableness
        All the relatives rave about the ineffable deliciousness of Aunt Meggie's cheesecake.

649. **necessitate** verb (nə ses′ə-tāt)
    to make necessary
      adj. necessitative
      noun necessitation
        The aggressive actions of the enemy necessitate our military buildup.

650. **colossal** adj. (kə-los′əl)
    enormous; huge
      adv. colossally
        Colossal ambitions may never be consummated (achieved).

651. **titanic** adj. (tī-tan′ik)
    huge; gigantic
      noun titan—a giant in any field of endeavor
        Titanic winds accompanied the tornado.

652. **prodigious** adj. (prə-dij′əs)
    1. huge
    2. amazing; extraordinary
      adv. prodigiously
      noun prodigiousness
        The establishment of an outer-space community would be a prodigious undertaking.

653. **ponderous** adj. (pon′dər-əs)
  1. heavy; huge; gigantic
  2. dull
     adv. ponderously
     noun ponderosity
     noun ponderousness
        A text on contractual law may be ponderous reading if you are not a lawyer.

654. **cohort** noun (kō′hôrt)
     a companion
        The manager went to lunch with a cohort.

655. **colleague** noun (kol′ēg)
     an associate; a fellow member of a profession
        noun colleagueship
           Why don't you and your colleague meet me for lunch?

656. **exhort** verb (ig′zôrt′)
     to urge; to recommend strongly; to advise
        adj. exhortative
        adj. exhortatory
        noun exhortation—an utterance that urges
        noun exhorter
           Did you exhort your men to work quickly?

657. **goad** verb (gōd)
     to incite; to urge
        noun goad—a stimulus; a prod
           The labor union threatened to goad a strike if the company refused to meet its demands.

658. **fledgling** noun (flej′ling)
    a beginner; a novice
        The young lawyer, a fledgling fresh out of
        law school, bungled his first case.


659. **neophyte** noun (nē′ə-fīt)
    a beginner; a novice
    adj. neophytic
        That slope is not for the neophyte skier.


660. **tyro** noun (tī′rō)
    a beginner; a novice
        Although just a tyro farmer, he produced
        an excellent crop.


661. **capitulate** verb (kə-pich′ōō-lāt)
    to surrender; to give up
    noun capitulator
    noun capitulation
        Facing inevitable (unavoidable) annihila-
        tion (destruction) the severely crippled
        army chose to capitulate.


662. **recapitulate** verb (rē′kə-pich′oo-lāt)
    to review; to summarize
    adj. recapitulative
    adj. recapitulatory
    noun recapitulation
        The professor would often recapitulate the
        prior morning's lecture.

663. **intransigent** adj. (in-tran′sə-jənt)
uncompromising; different
adv. intransigently
noun intransigency
noun intransigence
noun intransigentist
noun intransigent—one who is uncompromising
The intransigent architect designed build-
ings scorned by critics.

664. **indelible** adj. (in-del′ə-bəl)
incapable of being erased as from paper or mind
adj. indelibly
noun indelibility
noun indelibleness
Your charitableness has made an indelible
impression on all of us.

665. **equitable** adj. (ek′wə-tə-bəl)
fair; reasonable
adv. equitably
noun equitableness
The union reached what was termed an
equitable agreement with management.

666. **venal** adj. (vē-nəl)
willing to accept a bribe; subject to corrupt influ-
ences
adv. venally
noun venality
The venal judge accepted money to reduce
the criminal's sentence.

667. **venial** adj. (vē′nē-əl)
    excusable; pardonable
        adv. venially
        noun veniality
        noun venialness
            Shooting the burglar was ruled a venial act.


668. **besmirch** verb (bi-smûrch′)
    to soil; to stain; to sully
        noun besmirchment
        noun besmircher
            He tried to besmirch the good name of his
            rival.


669. **sully** verb (sul′ē)
    to soil; to stain; to besmirch
            It will be almost impossible to sully his
            good name.


670. **impregnable** adj. (im-preg′nə-bəl)
    incapable of being taken by force; strongly resis-
    tant; unyielding
        adv. impregnably
        noun impregnability
            The Indians attacked what proved to be an
            impregnable fort.


671. **infraction** noun (in-frak′shən)
    a violation
        verb infract—to violate
            The driver was unquestionably guilty of
            the speeding infraction.

672. **quixotic** adj. (kwik-sot′ik)
    ridiculously romantic or chivalrous; idealistic,
    but unpractical
        adv. quixotically
        noun quixoticism
            The quixotic sweepstakes winner felt he
            could now buy all of his dreams.


673. **iconoclast** noun (ī-kon′ə-klast)
    one who attacks cherished or established beliefs
    as being false
        adj. iconoclastic
        adv. iconoclastically
        noun iconoclasm
            The iconoclast believed we originated not
            from Adam and Eve, but from another
            solar system.


674. **gainsay** verb (gān′sā′)
    to deny; to contradict
        noun gainsayer
            "I'll gainsay every bit of information if my
            identity is made public," declared the in-
            formant.


675. **controvert** verb (kon′trə-vûrt)
    to deny; to argue against; oppose; contradict
        adj. controvertible
        adv. controvertibly
        noun controverter
            She found it difficult to controvert the
            evolutionist's theory.

676. **therapeutic** adj. (ther'ə-pyo͞o'tik)
  curative; healing
    adj. therapeutical
    adv. therapeutically
    noun therapeutics—a branch of science deal-
                          ing with the treatment of
                          sickness
    noun therapeutist
      Advocates of folklore medicine insist that a
      honey and vinegar mixture has therapeutic
      properties.

677. **lionize** verb (lī'ə-nīz)
  to treat as a celebrity
    noun lionization
    noun lionizer
      Everybody tended to lionize him even
      though he hadn't finished his first movie.

678. **plaudit** noun (plô'dit)
  an expression of praise; an expression of ap-
  proval
      The chairman of fund raising received
      a plaudit for his charitable efforts.

679. **accolade** noun (ak'ə-lād)
  an honor; an award
      Thank you for the accolade.

680. **paean** noun (pē'ən)
  a song of praise or joy
      The congregation sang a paean to the Lord.

681. **peon** noun (pē′ən)
  a laborer; an attendant
   noun peonage
   noun peonism
    Each peon was paid commensurate (proportionate) with the number of bushels of pickles he picked.

682. **plutocrat** noun (ploo′tə-krat)
  a wealthy person
    A fat little plutocrat had an imported calico cat that slept the day on a golden mat.

683. **insouciant** adj. (in-soo′sē-ənt)
  unconcerned; indifferent
   adv. insouciantly
   noun insouciance
    An insouciant attitude at election time is abominable (detestable).

684. **apathetic** adj. (ap′ə-thet′ik)
  unconcerned; indifferent
   adj. apathetical
   adv. apathetically
   noun apathy
    The farmers insinuated (suggested) that the president was apathetic over the plight (unfavorable condition) of the small farmer.

685. **habiliments** noun (hə-bil′ə-mənt)
  clothing; attire; garb
    We recognize policemen by the habiliments (usually plural) they wear.

686. **diurnal** adj. (dī-ûr′nəl)
daily; occurring each day
adv. diurnally
Due to a water shortage in that area of the country, people can no longer take their diurnal shower.


687. **momentous** adj. (mō-men′təs)
very important
adv. momentously
noun momentousness
New environmental policies have made this a momentous year for the pollution control industries.


688. **modicum** noun (mod′i-kəm)
a small amount
A modicum of praise was all the stimulus he needed to complete the laborious (difficult) task.


689. **discursive** adj. (dis-kûr′siv)
digressive; rambling; passing rapidly from one subject to another
adv. discursively
noun discursiveness
Senility (mental infirmity due to old age) often causes one to be discursive.

690. **distraught** adj. (dis-trôt′)
worried; agitated
The family was extremely distraught when
their only child was kidnapped.

691. **staid** adj. (stād)
sober; modest; steady
adv. staidly
noun staidness
The staid old teacher was recognized as
one of the best in the school system.

692. **sedate** adj. (si-dāt)
sober; composed; calm; unhurried; quiet
adj. sedative—soothing
adv. sedately
noun sedateness
noun sedation
noun sedative—a medicine that soothes pain
The sedate fireman calmly directed everybody out of the burning theater.

693. **stentorian** adj. (sten-tôr′ē-ən)
extremely loud
A stentorian voice boomed out over the
public address system.

694. **dilatory** adj. (dil′ə-tôr′ē)
tardy; slow; causing delay; lagging due to post-
poning
adv. dilatorily
noun dilatoriness
The contract was cancelled because of dilatory progress on the part of the builder.

695. **laggard** adj. (lag′ərd)
    slow; lagging due to laziness
      adv. laggardly
      noun laggard—one who lags
      noun laggardness
        A laggard old horse pulled the junkman's wagon around town.

696. **fiasco** noun (fē-as′kō)
    an absolute failure
        His house building venture turned into a fiasco.

697. **debacle** noun (dā-bäk′əl)
    a sudden collapse or breakdown
        The economic debacle created fears in the business community.

698. **futile** adj. (fyoo′təl)
    useless; ineffectual; done in vain
      adv. futilely
      noun futileness
      noun futility
        Arguing with a bigot (a person blindly attached to an idea) is futile.

699. **abortive** adj. (ə-bôr′tiv)
   failing
      adj. abortional
      adv. abortively
      noun abortiveness
      noun abortion—a failure
      verb abort—to fail to complete something
         The revolutionaries made an abortive attempt to overthrow the government.


700. **maudlin** adj. (môd′lin)
   1. excessively and tearfully emotional
   2. made foolish by liquor
         The intermission was a welcomed respite (relief) from the maudlin movie.

## Test 7

1. abortive  a. immortal  b. sentimental
   c. necessary  d. failing
2. accolade  a. honor  b. drink  c. felony
   d. boastfulness
3. allay  a. scare  b. attack  c. attribute  d. quiet
4. alleviate  a. avenge  b. send away  c. lessen
   d. annoy
5. apathetic  a. indifferent  b. stylish  c. vivid
   d. homesick
6. aplomb  a. favoritism  b. poise  c. gloom
   d. magic
7. apocryphal  a. conspicuously bad  b. false
   c. undecided  d. deserted
8. besmirch  a. stain  b. swindle  c. maim
   d. laugh
9. capitulate  a. destroy  b. give finishing touch
   c. sell  d. surrender
10. cohort  a. companion  b. bouquet
    c. double standard  d. denial
11. colleague  a. institution
    b. regional speech pattern  c. style
    d. associate
12. colossal  a. sporty  b. royal  c. fashionable
    d. enormous
13. comely  a. occasional  b. clear  c. attractive
    d. vile
14. controvert  a. rub hard  b. pull down  c. deny
    d. embezzle
15. debacle  a. uproarious spectacle  b. paranoia
    c. sudden collapse  d. short story
16. decimate  a. ease pain  b. push into limelight
    c. ban  d. destroy

17. dilatory  a. mournful  b. tardy  c. penetrable
    d. skilled
18. discursive  a. underhanded  b. enjoying
    c. punishing  d. rambling
19. distraught  a. consumptive  b. worried
    c. thrifty  d. weak
20. diurnal  a. short  b. rotten  c. daily  d. varied
21. dogmatic  a. overbearing  b. oversized
    c. furious  d. extremely formal
22. equitable  a. careless  b. like a horse  c. fair
    d. radiant
23. exhort  a. urge  b. plant deeply  c. entertain
    d. drive away
24. extenuating  a. idealistic  b. vigorous
    c. mitigative  d. unmanageable
25. fiasco  a. recovery  b. failure  c. abandonment
    d. repetition
26. fledgling  a. glutted state  b. tree branch
    c. old timer  d. beginner
27. foible  a. newspaper copy
    b. personal weakness  c. basement closet
    d. reward for bravery
28. futile  a. impractical  b. useless  c. fanatical
    d. inconsistent
29. gainly  a. oppressive  b. graceful  c. profitable
    d. high-up
30. gainsay  a. deny  b. speak eloquently
    d. charge ferociously forward  d. demolish
31. goad  a. break open  b. eat voraciously
    c. incite  d. withdraw quickly
32. habiliments  a. clothing  b. environment
    c. snacks  d. rehabilitation

33. haughty  a. weird  b. hospitable  c. arrogant
    d. shrewd
34. iconoclast  a. loyal servant
    b. one who thwarts progress
    c. one who attacks established beliefs
    d. deep thinker
35. idiosyncrasy  a. brief report  b. futuristic idea
    c. mannerism  d. insanity
36. impregnable  a. conquerable
    b. not conscientious  c. strongly resistant
    d. compact
37. impugn  a. attack statements or motives
    b. drive ahead  c. grant relief
    d. uplift spirits of another
38. incessant  a. continuous  b. unavailable
    c. cannot be reached  d. subsequent
39. indelible  a. motionless  b. neglected
    c. wordy and flowery
    d. incapable of being erased
40. ineffable  a. playful
    b. reasonable but incorrect  c. effective
    d. inexpressible
41. inept  a. unsuitable  b. easily accomplished
    c. untidy  d. minimum
42. infraction  a. frightening outcome
    b. act of friendship  c. evil behavior
    d. violation
43. insouciant  a. approaching  b. religious
    c. stagnant  d. unconcerned
44. intransigent  a. cannot be carried  b. nomadic
    c. uncompromising  d. suave
45. laggard  a. blushing  b. slow  c. sweltering
    d. mere

46. lionize  a. exert power  b. treat as celebrity
    c. fight fiercely  d. consume greedily
47. lissome  a. agile  b. casual  c. passing slowly
    d. doubtful
48. lithe  a. small  b. supple  c. limited
    d. unbounded
49. maudlin  a. colorless  b. excessively emotional
    c. overly committed  d. fearless
50. mince  a. tease  b. increase tempo  c. soften
    d. bring under control
51. mitigate  a. forget everything
    b. do something criminal  c. swindle
    d. make less severe
52. modicum  a. mediocre performance
    b. valueless object  d. training
    d. small amount
53. mollify  a. soothe  b. portray
    c. tarnish one's name  d. change
54. momentous  a. impromptu  b. tiny
    c. very important  d. abstract
55. moribund  a. accepted  b. dying  c. traveling
    d. prevalent
56. multifarious  a. holding fast  b. numerous
    c. having many enemies  d. vital parts
57. mundane  a. priestly  b. scholarly  c. abnormal
    d. routine
58. myriad  a. reflective  b. orderly  c. many
    d. lack of
59. necessitate  a. make necessary
    b. go by command  c. endure
    d. convert to something different
60. neophyte  a. beginner  b. sportsman
    c. newspaper reporter  d. strange condition

243

61. paean  a. laborer  b. large volume
    c. song of praise  d. small contribution
62. paragon  a. calmness  b. copy of plans
    c. model of excellence
    d. unintentional violation
63. peccable  a. capable of sinning  b. lawless
    c. unbecoming  d. fleeting
64. peccadillo  a. crazy idea  b. petty fault
    c. Mexican beverage  d. nasty argument
65. peon  a. song of joy  b. unique bargain
    c. laborer  d. inadequate
66. placate  a. calm  b. adjust  c. support  d. bribe
67. platonic  a. unsupportable
    b. devoid of sensual feeling  c. decent
    d. unkempt
68. plaudit  a. gimmick  b. command
    c. expression of distrust
    d. expression of praise
69. plausible  a. believable  b. disobedient
    c. exemplary  d. snobbish
70. pliant  a. limber  b. oily  c. outlandish
    d. unsatisfied
71. plutocrat  a. uncomprising bargainer
    b. wealthy person  c. dishonest politician
    d. authoritative personality
72. ponderous  a. awkward  b. rampaging
    c. fluent  d. heavy
73. posit  a. stimulate  b. select  c. place
    d. sharpen
74. potable  a. adhesive  b. forgivable
    c. bottomless  d. drinkable
75. pragmatic  a. bored with pleasure  b. indebted
    c. practical  d. having concern about economy

244

76. prodigious  a. eternal  b. noble  c. whimsical
    d. huge
77. prototype  a. original model  b. introduction
    c. state of bliss  d. distinguished guest
78. puissant  a. powerful  b. gigantic  c. capable
    d. cowardly
79. pulchritude  a. state of collapse
    b. impressive degree of knowledge  c. shock
    d. beauty
80. pusilanimous  a. brave  b. massive  c. timid
    d. cowardly
81. quixotic  a. not clearly defined  b. boisterous
    c. ridiculously romantic
    d. causing obstruction of justice
82. recapitulate  a. impede  b. reach decision
    c. review  d. thrust upon another
83. reciprocal  a. observable  b. overhanging
    c. mutual  d. legal and binding
84. rectify  a. erect a statue  b. correct
    c. construct  d. scandalize
85. rectitude  a. rightness  b. false excuse  c. thrift
    d. boastfulness
86. repository  a. place where things are put
    b. hide-out  c. contemporary play
    d. burial vault
87. sedate  a. slender  b. skeptical  c. sociable
    d. composed
88. spurious  a. not genuine  b. fully developed
    c. dizzy  d. noteworthy
89. staid  a. not fitting  b. commendable
    c. bungling  d. modest
90. stentorian  a. combative  b. extremely loud
    c. acting foolishly  d. tall

91. sully   a. act stupidly   b. hypnotize   c. forbid
    d. stain
92. supercilious   a. sullen   b. arrogant   c. abusive
    d. carefree
93. therapeutic   a. overemphasized
    b. coming into popularity   c. healing
    d. causing pain
94. titanic   a. plainly expressed   b. huge
    c. self-destructive   d. persistent
95. tranquil   a. sought after   b. calm
    c. having urge to travel   d. sharp-sighted
96. tyro   a. learned man   b. origin of something
    c. nearness   d. beginner
97. venal   a. unquestionable   b. pardonable
    c. out-of-date   d. subject to corrupt influences
98. venial   a. excusable   b. favorable
    c. sophisticated   d. willing to accept a bribe
99. viable   a. bending easily   b. simple
    c. capable of living normally   d. lively
100. virtuoso   a. musician   b. bad actor
    c. skilled person   d. level of society

# Test 7

## Answers

| | | | |
|---|---|---|---|
| 1. d | 26. d | 51. d | 76. d |
| 2. a | 27. b | 52. d | 77. a |
| 3. d | 28. b | 53. a | 78. a |
| 4. c | 29. b | 54. c | 79. d |
| 5. a | 30. a | 55. b | 80. d |
| 6. b | 31. c | 56. b | 81. c |
| 7. b | 32. a | 57. d | 82. c |
| 8. a | 33. c | 58. c | 83. c |
| 9. d | 34. c | 59. a | 84. b |
| 10. a | 35. c | 60. a | 85. a |
| 11. d | 36. c | 61. c | 86. a |
| 12. d | 37. a | 62. c | 87. d |
| 13. c | 38. a | 63. a | 88. a |
| 14. c | 39. d | 64. b | 89. d |
| 15. c | 40. d | 65. c | 90. b |
| 16. d | 41. a | 66. a | 91. d |
| 17. b | 42. d | 67. b | 92. b |
| 18. d | 43. d | 68. d | 93. c |
| 19. b | 44. c | 69. a | 94. b |
| 20. c | 45. b | 70. a | 95. b |
| 21. a | 46. b | 71. b | 96. d |
| 22. c | 47. a | 72. d | 97. d |
| 23. a | 48. b | 73. c | 98. a |
| 24. c | 49. b | 74. d | 99. c |
| 25. b | 50. c | 75. c | 100. c |

## SCORING

Correct answers
- 100-90=A (excellent)
- 89-80=B (good)
- 79-70=C (fair)
- 69-60=D (poor)
- 59- 0=E (Start over!)

Score before word study _____

Score after word study _____

# Index

# PRONUNCIATION KEY

| | | | | |
|---|---|---|---|---|
| a | map fat | sh | shut push | |
| ā | fāke lāy | t | tall pit | |
| â | âir bâre | th | thin cloth | |
| ä | bärb fäther | th̲ | there (th̲âr) another | |
| b | but tub | | (ə-nuth̲′ər) | |
| ch | chief leach | u | up dove (duv) | |
| d | dog sod | û | tûrn hûrt | |
| e | met end | yo͞o | use (yo͞oz) cute | |
| ē | ēve fee (fē) | | (kyo͞ot) | |
| f | filth calf | v | van hive | |
| g | go keg | w | waist away | |
| h | hate hear | y | yard yet | |
| i | it tin | z | zeal fuse (fyo͞oz) | |
| ī | īce nīght (nīt) | zh | treasure (trezh′er) | |
| j | jump hedge (hej) | | vision (vizh′ən) | |
| k | cat (kat) lake | (ə) | The schwa repre- | |
| l | low mule | | sents an unstress- | |
| m | my slim | | ed, weak or neutral | |
| n | now nice | | vowel as in: | |
| ng | sing long | | a aloud | |
| o | hot fox | | (ə-loud′) | |
| ō | nō ōdor | | e better | |
| ô | ôrder côrn | | (bet′ər) | |
| oi | coin toy (toi) | | i clarinet | |
| ou | out cloud | | (klar′ə-net′) | |
| o͞o | fo͞ol bo͞oze | | o felon | |
| o͝o | bo͝ok put (po͝ot) | | (fel′ən) | |
| p | pair stop | | u serious | |
| r | run try | | (sir′ē-əs) | |
| s | see mass | | | |